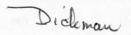

THE AMERICAN APPROACH
TO THE ARAB WORLD

THE AMERICAN
APPROACH TO
THE ARAB WORLD

by JOHN S. BADEAU

Published for the
Council on Foreign Relations
by
Harper & Row, Publishers
New York, Evanston, and London

The Council on Foreign Relations is a nonprofit institution devoted to the study of political, economic, and strategic problems as related to American foreign policy. It takes no stand, expressed or implied, on American policy.

The authors of books published under the auspices of the Council are responsible for their statements of fact and expressions of opinion. The Council is responsible only for determining that they should be presented to the public.

For a list of Council publications see pages 205-209.

THE AMERICAN APPROACH TO THE ARAB WORLD

Copyright © 1968 by Council on Foreign Relations, Inc.
*All rights reserved, including the right to reproduce
this book or any portion thereof in any form.
For information, address Harper & Row, Publishers, Incorporated
49 East 33rd Street, New York, N. Y. 10016*

FIRST EDITION

*Library of Congress catalog card number: 67-22494
Printed in the United States of America
Published by Harper & Row, Publishers, Incorporated*

A-S

Policy Books of the Council on Foreign Relations

For the past two decades the United States has been in search of policies in the Middle East that would protect its own interests and serve the cause of world peace. The record is not one of unmixed success. Some of the difficulties stem from the stresses, shifts and eruptions which have marked the local scene, especially among the Arabs at a time when they were simultaneously taken up with the struggles of political emancipation and social change and confronted with the fact of the State of Israel. Some arise from considerations of American domestic politics. The problems have remained intractable and often imperfectly understood. Drastic changes in the situation in the Middle East, including so shattering an event as the Arab-Israel war of June 1967, have neither dispelled them nor removed the need for clear and effective American policies. On the contrary, it is more than ever necessary that this country work out an adequate approach to the Arab world.

This is the subject which John S. Badeau set for himself in undertaking this volume in the Council's series of Policy Books. Begun before the hostilities of June 1967, it rests on the whole history of American-Arab relations. The events of the past year, which are fully taken into account, provided a timely test of the analysis and the conclusions. Professor of Modern Arabic Studies and Director of Columbia University's Middle East Institute, combining long experience in the area with an inside knowledge of American diplomacy during recent years as American Ambassador to the United Arab Republic, Dr. Badeau is uniquely qualified to write this book. Like others of the Council's Policy Books, it presents the personal views of the author on major issues against a background of relevant information clearly and briefly presented.

The author had the benefit of the advice of a small group which met for a day at the Council to review and discuss his manuscript. He and the Council are grateful to the following, who either attended the review meeting or gave their views and comments directly to him: Richard H. Nolte (Chairman), William J. Barnds, Col. Michael J. L. Greene, USA, Raymond Hare, Alan Horton, Harry N. Howard, J. C. Hurewitz, Joseph E. Johnson, Don Peretz, William R. Polk, Nadav Safran, Hedrick Smith, Harrison Symmes, Theodore Tannenwald, R. Bayly Winder, Charles W. Yost, and T. Cuyler Young. This is, however, Professor Badeau's book. Neither the Council nor any group has responsibility for its statements of fact or opinion. The Council does take responsibility for the decision to publish it as a contribution to thinking on one of the most important, and most baffling, problems of American foreign policy.

JOHN C. CAMPBELL
Editor

Preface

A verse of doggerel sometimes heard from children playing in the streets of an Arab city runs:

> You can say what you like, and I'll tell you flat
> He is not that, he is not that.*

Anyone undertaking to write a brief description of conditions and problems in the Middle East and the Arab world must share this uncertainty. Despite its superficial unity, the area is so diverse and is in the midst of such constant change that generalizations about it are difficult to make without neglecting some pertinent factor. This is the more true when the treatment must be limited in length. The author readily admits to having excluded, or given only brief treatment to, aspects both of American policy and of the Arab world which deserve fuller consideration.

The object of this study is not to chronicle all the facets and details of American policies toward each of the states which together comprise the Arab world. It is rather to consider the general framework of facts, objectives, and instruments within which policy judgments have been, and will continue to be, made—hence the "American approach" to the Arab world rather than "American policy" toward it. It is not written to propose a policy on Arab affairs, partly because no single policy can embrace the nebulous concept of an Arab world, partly because specific policies toward individual Arab countries must vary with the time, type of problem, and individual interest

---

* A popularization of the credo of some Muslim theologians that God can only be described in negative terms, apart from His existence, unity and power.

involved. What is more constant is a sense of direction—the "approach" with which this study attempts to deal. The study is intended to throw light on how that approach came into being, what it has involved, and some of the directions in policy it may indicate for the future.

For this purpose, some definition in geographical terms is in order. In point of fact, the Arab world runs from Morocco on the Atlantic Ocean in the west to the states of the Arabian peninsula on the Indian Ocean in the east. It is divided into the North African states—from Libya westward—and the eastern Arab states—from Egypt to the Indian Ocean. In one sense, all are equally parts of the Arab world in that they share an Arab consciousness, are historically rooted in the period of Arab empire, and have been members of the League of Arab States. But from another viewpoint North Africa has a recognizable personality of its own. Fronting on Europe, for some time closely tied to France and French influences (with the exception of Libya), its political and international problems have their own characteristics. In this study, attention is focused on the eastern Arab world, although some references are made to the North African Arab states when an observation legitimately applies to them.

Within the eastern Arab world, equal attention has not been given to every state. This is due partly to limitations of length and partly to the nature of the problems discussed. To some readers the United Arab Republic (Egypt) may seem to occupy too much of the writer's attention. If this is true, it may be a reflection of the fact that the author's longest residence was in Egypt, and it was in Cairo that he had his diplomatic experience. However, apart from this fact, the U.A.R. is the leading state in the eastern Arab world and necessarily has occupied an important role both in intra-Arab affairs and in American foreign policy toward the area. The United States has probably had more policy problems with Egypt (since the revolution of 1952) than with any other Arab state, and these problems have frequently affected its policy toward the others. Moreover, many of the most typical problems of the eastern Arab world come to sharp focus in Egyptian life and policies and can be identified most readily there. Thus the U.A.R. may serve the same role in a study of the Arab world that abnormal psychology does to the beginning student of psychology—to present in exaggerated form (and therefore more clearly defined) some of the major attributes which characterize less extreme situations.

An able observer of Iranian affairs once said: "If anyone claims he knows what will happen in Iran, he is misinformed." To a large degree the same is true of the Arab world. It is impossible to prophesy what the future holds, either for the Arab states or for the United States in dealing with them. The author does not attempt to prophesy; merely to observe and in some cases to speculate.

J.S.B.

New York
September 1967

Contents

Contents

THE AMERICAN APPROACH
TO THE ARAB WORLD

Chapter I

The Role of the United States

In few of its postwar policies has the United States been more ill at ease than in dealing with the Arab world. Bearing responsibilities alien to its past experience, linked with allies who were once the colonial masters of the area, suspect in the eyes of the Arabs themselves, the United States has never quite made up its mind what course to pursue. For two decades it has felt its way through the recurrent crisis of the area, seldom entirely failing in its objectives, yet equally seldom quite reaching them. Bold initiative and sustained consistency have not been the hallmark of its approach.

Critics are not wanting to proclaim the cause of this difficulty. Domestically there is a body of opinion which for varying reasons maintains that the United States has been too soft with the Arabs. "Force is all they understand," it has been argued, and sufficient force would have curtailed Nasser, imposed an Arab-Israel peace, and more successfully contested the Soviet position. Among some European allies a variant of the same charge has been made: if the United States had accepted whole-heartedly its role as successor to British and French imperial power, cooperated consistently to protect the remnants of that power, and used its economic and political position to induce Arab respect for Western interests, all would be well.

Others argue in the opposite vein. They see the rising nationalism of the Arab world as the great opportunity for the United States to secure an ally in a critical area, and failure to respond to Arab aspirations as the basic cause for the equivocal American record. Arab nationalists also have an explanation for American ineffectiveness. They see the United States so held in fee to its partners, the former colonial powers, and to the supporters of Israel that it cannot pursue an independent policy based upon its own national interests. Furthermore, its stake in petroleum has driven the United States into an alliance with the more traditional states of the area rather than with the forces of change and progress which many Arabs see as the wave of the future.

Implicit in such criticisms are divergent assumptions as to what the role of the United States in the Arab world is or should be. "Hardline" Americans imply that it is essentially a policing function, responsible for keeping communism under control, preserving law and order, and intervening to prevent or end conflicts. Some European powers would have the United States fill the power vacuum which allegedly is always pulling some outside force into the Middle East. Arab nationalists envision the proper American role as an ally of the Arab cause, identifying American interests with a strong, free, and progressive Arab world.

But the American role is not thus simply defined. Not only has it emerged by unplanned and pragmatic development, but it operates on a scene that is different from the earlier situations on which so many of the arguments concerning it are based. Both in its internal character and its external relations, the Arab world has been changing constantly since the United States first began to assume responsibilities toward it at the end of the Second World War. What may have been possible at the end of the war or prior to the Egyptian-Soviet arms deal in 1955 and the Suez crisis in 1956 may not be possible today; and what could not be done in the first Arab enthusiasm for the new Soviet connection may now be tried with greater hope of success. No cliché is more misleading than that of the unchanging Middle East, no policy more futile than one which confines the future course within the limits of past solutions.

To define the American role involves a review of the process by which the United States became the principal Western actor on the Arab scene. Prior to the Second World War, the United States traditionally held aloof from active participation in Middle Eastern affairs. Early in the nineteenth century it had briefly acted in the area in its Barbary Coast campaigns, and at one time President Monroe was pressed to consider declaring war against Turkey to aid the Greeks in their struggle for independence. But as the United States became preoccupied with its own pressing problems of national development, it became less active in international affairs. In the Middle East it accepted the growing position of Great Britain and France. This led to a policy of American non-involvement in the area which was breached only when specific American interests were at stake—as in the parceling out of petroleum resources at the end of the First World War. Between the two world wars the United States sought to stay clear of Middle East involvements, by recognizing the French and British dominant position and carrying on only a limited diplomacy with the emerging Middle East states.

As the Second World War ended there seemed to be no pressing reason to alter this policy. Great Britain emerged from the conflict with its position in the Arab world apparently still strong. The British had played the leading military role in that theater and through the Middle East Supply Center had maintained their economic relations with the Arab states. In Egypt, they had a strong position, buttressed by British troops. In Jordan and Iraq there were friendly regimes brought to power or supported by Great Britain. In Libya, Syria, and Lebanon British action had been a factor in securing local independence from other European powers, and it was not unreasonable to expect some gratitude for this contribution. There seemed to be no reason why the United States should not continue to stay out of Arab affairs, relying on the British presence to maintain protection of Western and American interests.

But British strength was more apparent than real. The postwar weakness of Great Britain made it difficult to sustain its commitments, let alone meet new challenges. The deepening impasse in

Palestine, ending in British withdrawal and the outbreak of the Arab-Israel conflict, contributed heavily to the alienation of Arab opinion from the British. In many countries a new generation of nationalists began to come to power, and for them a British connection was no longer the basic assumption of independence and national development.

It was the growing pressure of Soviet activity in the Middle East which challenged this weakness and forced the United States to assume its first responsibilities in the area. Initially, these responsibilities were not undertaken in the Arab world but in the northern tier states of Iran, Turkey, and Greece where Soviet action threatened the stability of existing governments. To meet this situation, the United States, through the Truman Doctrine of 1947, took the momentous step of becoming the prime support for the defense establishments of Greece and Turkey, since it was apparent that Great Britain no longer had the resources to do so.

Once its tradition of aloofness from Middle Eastern affairs was broken, the United States was faced with recurring British requests for cooperation and help. At no point was it suggested that Great Britain should abdicate her Middle East role; rather it was that America should become a junior partner with her. Thus, the proposed Middle East Defense Organization (1951–52) was to have largely British military leadership. The Baghdad Pact (1955), although stemming from American rather than British initiative, was joined by Britain as a means of maintaining her position in the area. With Britain, the United States assisted in the creation of independent Libya (1951), and initiated the Tripartite Declaration (1950) in which the two powers and France guaranteed the Arab-Israel borders and undertook to control the supply of arms to both sides. Not until the announcement of the Eisenhower Doctrine in 1957 did the United States assume independent guarantees to the Arab world.

The basic cause for these growing commitments was not an American interest in the Arab world per se, nor a desire to take over the British position. It was part of the problem of global defense against Soviet might in which its strategic location gave the Middle East a highly significant role. At the beginning of the period the United States judged the Soviet threat to be mainly overt—a view strongly reinforced by the outbreak of the Korean War. The United States thus saw its role chiefly as building a military bulwark against Soviet occupation or control—a role which made support of military establishments, conclusion of defense treaties, and guarantees of protection the basic dimensions of American responsibility.

This view of the Soviet threat as chiefly military was sharply challenged by the Egyptian arms deal of 1955. With that deal the Soviets vaulted over the northern defense tier, which the West had erected with so much hope, and appeared on the Arab scene by the invitation of an Arab nationalist state. The invitation was proof that the monopoly of Western control of the Arab world was gone, and that Arab nationalism was a force affecting both Western interests and Soviet ambitions. In the aftermath of this discovery, the United States was forced to reconsider its role, now that direct military support did not fully answer the problem of Middle East security.

Suez and After

The definition of that role was made more urgent by the final collapse of the British position in the crisis which followed nationalization of the Suez Canal Company in 1956. As a result of the ill-conceived and ineptly mounted Anglo-French military action, the last tie between Great Britain and Egypt was broken. Whatever hope there may have been for continued cooperation between the two countries, as set by the 1954 agreement covering the withdrawal of British forces from the Suez area, was blasted. The Suez Canal became a purely Egyptian responsibility. For the first time in many centuries, Egypt stood as a fully sovereign state, unoccupied by any foreign force, successfully demonstrating her independence against Western pressures that controlled her destiny since the British occupation in 1882. Historically, British policy had sought to develop a partnership with Arab forces. "Satellite" may be too strong a word for this relationship, but it did envision a connection so strong that the senior partner could rely on its junior's support and acquiescence whenever British interests were at stake. That policy now became impossible.

Moreover, the action of the United Nations in forcing an end to the invasion reinforced a new element of world power in the Middle East. The international community served notice that it would not place its interests in world peace at the mercy of individual great-power policies. The effectiveness of U.N. action, of course, owed a great deal to the decision of the United States to oppose the Anglo-French venture—to say nothing of threats from the Soviet Union. The tacit agreement of prewar years that a British special position in the Arab world served general Western interests no longer held. Not only did the failure of the invasion show that Great Britain was unable to enforce its position by direct action, but also the results of that action threatened, rather than served, the Western position.

Nor was the effect of the invasion less profound in the Arab world itself. Despite varying degrees of distrust between individual Arab countries and revolutionary Egypt, the Arab world applauded and supported Egyptian resistance. In Arab eyes, the British imperialist had shown he had not changed his spots and would use force if he could get away with it. But now Egypt had emerged as the champion of Arab self-determination, demonstrating that the British hold on Arab life could be challenged successfully.

Western observers often overlook or underestimate the continuing effects of the 1956 experience on the Arab mind. Seven years after the event, suspicion of British motives was still strong. British moves in Africa, Cyprus, and Aden in 1962–63 were read as attempts to re-establish a dominant British position. The mood of the Arab world was not unlike that of the United States during the War of 1812, which was popularly seen as proof that Great Britain had never reconciled herself to the independence of the American colonies and would move against them if she saw the opportunity. Moreover, many Arabs, especially the military leadership in Egypt, were convinced that, given the opportunity, Israel would "try it again." Caught off guard with its military establishment unprepared and sustaining a stunning defeat, the Nasser regime began to build up its armed strength with Soviet assistance, so that "next time" they would be ready. Thus 1956 became the backdrop against which the Arab attitudes and actions of 1967 developed. In many ways the West forgot 1956— or concluded that its disastrous lesson had been marked and inwardly digested by the Arabs. But the Arab world did not forget, and the lesson they read was that military strength and a prompt, forestalling action were the essentials against a recurrence of overt action by an aggressive Israel supported by the West.

The 1956 invasion was the most disastrous piece of postwar Western diplomacy in the Middle East. Based on false estimates of Western unity, British and French capacity, and the strength of Arab nationalism, it formed a watershed in the relations of the West with the Arab world. The Soviets emerged from the crisis with enhanced reputation and a closer identification with Arab aspirations. The Western powers emerged from it with tarnished reputation and facing a situation in which even limited cooperation with Arab states was difficult to maintain. Britain and France had failed in their resort to force to protect their interests, and any other Western power would also fail if it pursued a similar course. The British collapse may have formed a power vacuum in the area—but the vacuum was not one which could be filled by some new power assuming an identical role.

There are those who still argue that American policy in the Suez crisis was mistaken. Had the United States acquiesced in, if not actively supported, the British move, Egypt, they contend, would have been brought to heel, the Nasser regime ended, and the Suez Canal returned to international control. But this is only a wishful misreading of the situation. Had the Anglo-French action taken place a few days after the nationalization of the Canal, it is probable that Egypt would have bowed to the inevitable, and the international community would have been faced with a *fait accompli* it could not undo. But what was possible a week after nationalization was not possible three months later when the affair had become an international *cause célèbre* and the various power factors had time to align themselves.

In any case, there is no evidence that any substitute for the Nasser regime could have been found that would have been fundamentally different in character and permanently more subservient to Western interests. Nasser might have been overthrown, but the results would ultimately have been to evoke a revived and more radical Egyptian nationalism. The Arab world, and probably most of the new emerging nations, would have been driven even further from the Western camp. More important, it is possible that the United Nations would have gone the way of the League of Nations when it proved unwilling to take an effective stand in the Italian invasion of Ethiopia.

Thus the Suez debacle forced the United States to face a new and more consciously chosen role in the Arab world. No longer was it possible to act chiefly as an auxiliary to British policy. Not only was Britain unable to provide the chief element of strength, but the United States had taken an irrevocable step in disassociating itself from British policy in an hour of major crisis. By supporting, in conjunction with the Soviets, the United Nations action to halt the invasion, America in effect declared its independence of British policy and accepted responsibility for choosing a line of action based upon its own estimate of the situation. This was a far cry from the days of the Truman Doctrine when the United States acted because Britain could not act. Now it acted because Britain had acted—and acted in a way which America considered a danger to its own and to general international interests.

The situation which the United States faced in the Arab world after Suez contained several new factors. Inescapably the United States found itself custodian of the general Western position. In consequence, the American role was both independent and limited. It was independent in that it was no longer chiefly a supplement to the traditional position of European powers but rested on American determination of interests and policies. No Western power could successfully adopt a major policy toward the Arab world which conflicted with that of the United States. European policies had become supplemental; American policies, basic. But this independence was limited in that the United

States was not acting solely for itself. It was subject to pressure from its allies and pursued general objectives which it shared with them, notably access to oil and defense against Soviet expansion.

The United States, as the custodian per se for a complex of international concerns far wider than those faced by any foreign power in the past, had to decide which of these concerns were truly basic and vital to the West. Was the British air base in Libya or the naval base at Aden so essential to the defense of the free world that the United States should risk a rupture of its Arab relations to defend them? Was the threat of closer relations between the United Arab Republic and East Germany sufficiently serious in its relation to the Western alliance to warrant the withdrawal of American aid from the U.A.R.? There was a natural tendency among American allies to seek U.S. support for all their national interests, including commercial investments, the property of private citizens, and privileged positions resulting from earlier colonial days. The United States could not undertake all these, yet it could not summarily dismiss them and act only in reference to narrowly defined American interests. In its new role of responsibility, it had to develop criteria for judging its various interests, both to avoid being used as the cat's paw in every dispute between a Western and an Arab state and to identify those interests most essential to the strength and security of the free world.

At the beginning of American responsibility in the Middle East, there were those who believed that the United States could come forward as a new and acceptable influence *from* the West, without being identified by local nationalism as *of* the West. In a sense it hoped to become a "third force" in Arab life, offering the values of Western culture and development still sought by many Arabs without being identified as part of the Western colonial system. A century of noninvolvement in Arab affairs, a long record of philanthropic contribution in education, health and social work made this seem a reasonable hope. But in the Arab world, as in other areas, the American hope of coming forward with a non-European image while retaining a European connection was proved futile. As the United States emerged as the chief guardian of Western interests, its policies were generally seen by the Arabs as a new facet of the control they had so long experienced—the great exception being American action in the Suez Canal crisis. It was not only that the United States had often to act in the interests of its Western allies, but that the nature of American interests led it to pursue policies identified with European control in the past. These factors led the United States (especially during the Dulles period) to support pro-Western regimes in the Middle East or to attempt to bring such regimes to power. Alleged actions by the CIA in Syria, Egypt, and Iran are often cited by Arabs as clear evidence of this "imperialism."

The American interest in stability of the Arab world sometimes led it to the support of traditional monarchies whose position was based upon a landlord and merchant elite rather than upon the greater assent of the commonality. Many Arabs believed that such elite groups keep their power against the best interests of the citizenry by cooperating with the West through petroleum sales, subsidies, and political favoritism. Were American and other Western support to be withdrawn from such regimes, it was argued, they would quickly fall. This is to say that in its new role American action was often interpreted as directed toward the same objectives as those pursued by Britain and France in the past. The United States found that it bore some of the onus of European colonial days, even though it eschewed any imperial ambitions of its own.

The Soviet Presence

A further factor determining the American role was the presence and influence of another major foreign power in the area— the Soviet Union. To be sure, this power had operated in the Middle East since the end of the war, and was the chief cause for the assumption of American responsibilities in the region. But with the 1955 Egyptian arms deal, the Suez debacle, and the ensuing collapse of the British position, the Soviet presence took on a new and more permanent character. By political support for

Egyptian resistance to the West, the Soviets entered the Arab world not through the threat of force (as in Iran at the end of the war) or the support of local subversive movements (as in Greece) but by its identification with the aspirations of Arab nationalism. The Soviets offered a substitute for a European connection and were accepted on this basis in Egypt and some other Arab countries. Even where Soviet offers were not accepted, they could be used as a threat to counterbalance unpalatable Western pressure. As one Egyptian put it: "The West no longer has us in a corner. We are now in a corridor and if you press us too hard we can always come out at the other end."

This "other end" involved a variety of possible Arab-Soviet connections. The earliest was the supply of arms. Until 1955, Arab armaments were supplied principally by Great Britain and France. Their size, type and rate of increase was in Western hands and could be regulated by Western interests. Now that power of regulation largely disappeared. The United Arab Republic, Syria, and Iraq turned to the Soviet Union with a resulting large increase in their military capacity and an absence of inhibitions in its use against Western interests, except insofar as the Soviets might restrain them. When the United States began to emerge as the principal Western power in the Arab world, it could conceivably have taken on the role of arms supplier in an attempt to stalemate or diminish the Soviet position in the field. But to do so would have plunged the United States deeply into the conflicts and tensions of the area, of which the Arab-Israel conflict not only is the most continuous but also arouses the greatest agitation of both American and Arab public opinion.

The "other end" also included a new economic connection between the Soviet Union and the Arab world which was not easily broken. The arms deal involved the Arab states in the problem of payment and opened the way for barter deals with the Soviets which were extended into nonmilitary fields of development. The Aswan High Dam is merely a dramatic example of Soviet assistance in developmental projects and industrial expansion, based upon barter credits.

Concomitant with the supply of arms and aid has been the

penetration through technical contacts. Soviet credits were naturally utilized for projects involving Soviet machinery, materials and technical processes. The High Dam necessitated a continuing Soviet team of some 800 technicians to work with Egyptian engineers. Whatever the political effect may be, the technical effect has been profound. Not only has it led to close association with Soviet technicians and their methods, but it also requires Arab technicians who could operate and service Soviet equipment. So long as this equipment is in use, it will be necessary for the Arab states which have it to train a number of technicians under Soviet auspices.

The position of the Soviets as the suppliers of arms, aid, and techniques has been reflected in some Arab positions and actions in the councils of the United Nations. Under colonial rule and during the early years of independence the relation between an Arab state and the international community was through, or largely controlled by, the "protecting" Western power. With the disappearance of this link, the Arabs were offered a substitute for their old political dependence on the West in the Soviet international role. It was a substitute with its own measure of dependence, for Soviet involvement in internal Arab developments was of such importance that the Soviets could bring pressure for the support of their views. That pressure has not been as successful as many Westerners predicted or as the Soviet leaders hoped, but it has been a factor in the international attitudes of some Arab states which cannot be lightly dismissed. The clear, persistent and sustained Soviet voice in the Security Council on behalf of all the Arab states involved in the June 1967 Arab-Israel conflict demonstrated how far the international-diplomatic role of the U.S.S.R. can involve Arab interests and be used to support Arab causes.

Thus, at every level of its relations with the Arab world—military, economic, technical, international—the United States faced the presence of a competing great power which in fact or in potential challenged the Western position. This was a new situation for Western interests in the Arab world. After the Anglo-French rivalries at the turn of the century and the German *Drang nach Osten* on the eve of the First World War, there was no serious great-power competition in the area. During the past half century the chief opposition to the Anglo-French position came from Arab national movements, which were internal and localized forces. Nationalism is still the most powerful and ubiquitous anti-Western force in the Arab world, but today it is a nationalism which can be encouraged, supported, and sometimes manipulated by external powers challenging Western interests. In this situation, the kind and degree of pressure the United States can mount in its role of protecting Western interests is sharply limited.

But Soviet pressure on the Arab world also is limited by the same factor of a competing great-power presence. To be sure, the so-called pro-Soviet Arab states do not directly appeal to the United States to counter major Soviet pressure, but the American presence and the intent of American interests is such that even without appeal they count on counterbalancing Western moves. The assumption on which some Arab states have felt free to develop close ties with the Soviets in such vital matters as the supply of arms and large economic assistance has been that if these connections should lead to the brink of Soviet control, the United States would act to prevent the tumble over the edge. Hence the surprisingly muted Arab criticism of the "imperialist" Sixth Fleet in the Mediterranean which is recognized (although seldom publicly admitted) as a final barrier against overt Soviet action. In more immediate issues, American aid could be sought (though not always obtained) as a counterbalance to Soviet offers.

While many Americans may react against such tactics as a form of blackmail, they undoubtedly have worked. Thus Jordan obtained tanks and aircraft from the United States (despite the announced American policy of not being an arms supplier in the Arab world) in part to offset Soviet arms to the U.A.R. In part, too, the alternative to American weapons might well have been Soviet arms, which Syria and the U.A.R. have urged on other Arab states to secure uniformity of equipment under the Arab Unified Command created in 1964.

In a larger sense, the Arab states, like many others, have enjoyed an expanded area of independent action because of the nuclear stalemate. The issues in which Arab policies or problems could generate an East-West crisis have been reduced. Neither the United States nor the Soviet Union will pursue a policy in the Arab world to the point of an inevitable major clash with the other unless the most serious national interest is at stake. Knowing this, Arab governments can oscillate between the two poles with far less fear of being captured by either or of destroying their independence by setting off a major conflict. They cannot count, however, on the unchanging nature of East-West polarity. Should it decline in the Middle East, as it has in some other areas, they would lose some of their bargaining power; and in the last analysis, they cannot be sure that either great power at a time of crisis would see the Arab interest as its own—as Soviet actions (in contrast to words) showed in the 1967 Arab-Israel confrontation.

Thus the role of the United States since 1956 has come a long way since the Truman Doctrine in 1947. It is the principal guardian of Western interests, yet that guardianship is hedged about by limits unknown in the colonial era. The Soviet presence in the Arab world, the sovereign status of the Arab states, the latitude of Arab action produced by nuclear stalemate, and the ability of the international community to develop quickly a climate of opinion have given a different setting to Western interests. It is within this setting, realistically appraised and accepted, that the United States has had to develop its foreign policy toward the Arab world.

Chapter II

The Nature of American
Interests

In developing its role in the Arab world, the United States has had to define its basic interests in the area. Foreign policy is, or ought to be, an instrument for defining and furthering national interests. Uncertainty as to what those interests are inevitably leads to uncertain policy formulation. The vagaries and frustrations of American policy toward the Arab world are due in part to confusion as to what American interests really are.

Some of them, it has been noted, are Western and international, not narrowly American. How to disentangle their essential character as international concerns from their incidental relation to past colonial policies has been a major problem. Adequate defense of the Arab world in relation to the security of the free world is obviously an international interest, as it is an American national interest, but to what extent does that interest involve protection for the remnants of the British position in Aden and the Persian Gulf, or for maintaining them as an American responsibility if and when the British depart?

Moreover, in the process of transfer of international responsibility from British or French power, such interests (however validly defined) took on a new character because they were set in a new situation. The cold war struggle in its varying stages, the global nature of security and defense, the position of the United States in the Western alliance, the multiplication of American commitments in nearly every part of the world, and the sovereign status of the Arab states have affected their substance and form. Stability and tranquility in the Arab world were international concerns in colonial days and remain international concerns today —but both the forces threatening them and the instruments for promoting them have changed radically.

A further difficulty arises from the tension between particular interests in specific Arab countries and more general interests in the Arab world and the Middle East. Still a nebulous term, "Arab world" does not correspond to a political entity with which diplomatic relations can be maintained; it does not even denote a common denominator which binds Arab states together in all circumstances. General movements are under way throughout the Arab world which affect international interests and must be a cause for international concern. But these movements take different forms in different countries, making it difficult to have a consistent area-wide policy toward them. Even when such a policy is possible, particular interests in specific countries may conflict with it.

It can be argued, for example, that the Western interest in stability and progress should result in a policy of supporting progressive—in some cases radical—movements throughout the Arab world, so that the West may be identified with the emerging future rather than the decaying past—if its pattern can be discerned. Yet in some Arab countries where particular American and Western interests are strong, the passage from traditionalism to modernity may wreck the stability of the existing order in which the American interest is set. In these circumstances, particular interests in the specific country tend to take precedence. This is partly a time factor. Particular interests in specific countries are immediate, or at best short-term, while many interests general to the area are long-term, connected with movements, conditions and policies which will bear fruit only in a remote future. How to define general American interest in the Arab world, yet allow for the reality of specific short-term interest, is a constant problem.

The Context of Global Responsibilities

Before defining American interests in the Arab world, we must consider the general framework of global objectives in which they are set. The United States did not assume its first major responsibilities in the Middle East (the Truman Doctrine of 1947) merely because Turkey and Greece were set in a strategic area. The move was a reflection of two general objectives which became, and have continued, central to American policy from that time.

The first of these has been to contain Soviet-Communist expansion wherever it may threaten. This containment has been based on both military-political and ideological factors. Politically the U.S.S.R. and its "camp" represents a major and competing center of global power whose expansion could threaten the security of the United States and the non-Communist world. To prevent the further acquisition of territory and positions of strength by the Soviets has been judged a necessity for global security. At the same time, the implied threat has been ideological. The philosophy and forms of society produced by the Communist system are seen as inimical to the freedom and independence of other nations and to the kind of international order in which they can live with security. While the stance of peaceful co-existence which has emerged from the cold war may make possible some mutual accommodation of interests, it is an accommodation which could be upset by any substantial expansion of Soviet power or of the Communist system.

The second objective has been the maintenance of general stability on the world scene. Instability is dangerous because it breeds tensions and disputes which may escalate into major conflicts or place difficult peace-keeping tasks on the world community—as witness Cyprus, the Congo, and Yemen. Instability among nations also complicates and interrupts the internal development of emergent countries, for which economic, political and social progress is the precondition for a hopeful future. Local disputes and radical attempts at change may also provide a tempting setting for Soviet-Communist activity, to which the non-Communist world will have to acquiesce or otherwise undertake commitments to curtail. As the principal non-Communist world power, such commitments would rest most heavily on the United States. Stability is thus necessary if America is to keep its commitments from multiplying to a point where its capacity is overstrained.

Both global objectives have put their stamp on American policy toward the Middle East and the Arab world. As a region contiguous with the southern borders of Russia, opening onto warm water and occupying a strategic position, it has attracted Russian attention since at least the beginning of the nineteenth century. The continuation of this historic interest under Soviet auspices was demonstrated in Soviet negotiations with Germany in 1940 and even more clearly in Stalin's moves at the close of the Second World War against Iran, Turkey, and Greece. The containment of Soviet-Communist expansion has thus had a particular relevance to the Middle East and has been a continuing element in American policy toward the area.

The maintenance of stability has also been a pervasive concern in the Middle East. Its nationalism was among the earliest in colonial areas and could be expected to intensify after the war. Radical reforms in Turkey and Iran during the inter-war period were warnings that other traditional systems in the area might follow the same path. The mounting tension of the Arab-Zionist dispute contained a potential for conflict which could reach far beyond the borders of Palestine. The Middle East had been an important theater of war, with all the disruption and frustration of local life that continuing military occupation brings. Threats to the existing order as it emerged from the war were inevitable. The general American concern for stability thus had special pertinence to the situation in the Middle East.

Yet, important as these global objectives are, they have not provided sufficient guidance for formulating a detailed foreign policy toward the Middle East because their content, when carefully scrutinized, is nebulous. Is every expansion of the Soviet position, every gain in influence, equally a security threat? Some expansion has brought the Soviets at least as many liabilities as assets. What appeared to be a strong position at the outset has sometimes turned out to be weak or inconsequential at the end. During the 1950s, some Americans bewailed the "loss" of Afghanistan through Soviet arms sales and the blandishments of the "gold dust twins" (Bulganin and Khrushchev). Yet a decade later Afghanistan still retained a sturdy independence, and the Russians had not been able to build a dominant position.

The same considerations affect the threat of new advances of communism. A few years ago Indonesia appeared to be approaching rapidly a point of no return, with some form of indigenous (and possibly Chinese-backed) communism imminent. Yet an overt move to establish Communist domination precipitated a popular revolt which within a short time swept that threat away, even to the point of taking power out of the hands of President Sukarno.

Moreover, it is difficult to determine in what sense a radical or revolutionary movement is indeed "Communistic" and whether it will be controlled by Moscow or Peking. Communism as a system has itself changed and diversified in the decades since the war. Soviet communism has come under attack by the "purist" Chinese theoreticians as being communism no longer. In the East European states, communism has been altered to serve local problems and local needs so that it is no longer possible to speak with accuracy of "a Communist system" which spreads across the world.

The objective of supporting stability is likewise nebulous. Can international and internal stability be separated? If preserving stability means the containment of those forces which challenge existing political structures, it means in effect the maintenance of the *status quo* in a given country or area. But this is often both impossible and undesirable. The forces of change are ubiquitous and pressing. Containing them may only lead to a violent explosion in the future. True stability in some cases is only possible if change takes place. To oppose every attempt to alter the existing order on the thesis that this poses a threat to stability may be self-defeating. The objective of maintaining world stability must thus encompass the desirability and possibility of change, the chief question being not whether change should take place, but how can it be made as orderly and productive as possible.

Thus the global objectives have not been sufficient to supply a detailed American foreign policy toward the Arab world. They have often set the mood of the American response to area problems, providing a frame of reference in which judgments on Soviet moves and Arab radical developments are made. One result has been at times to focus American attention and policy too narrowly on containing the Soviets and inhibiting revolutionary movements in the Arab world, without giving due weight to other factors in the situation. What is needed is a more specific definition of American interests in the area, which, while connected with and reflecting global objectives, are the immediate guideposts of a foreign policy.

Primary Interests

In this study, the term "interest" is given a limited meaning, being used for those concerns which so closely affect American security, in itself and as related to the non-Communist world, that they involve commitments for their defense. In this sense, the interests of the United States in the Arab world are relatively few and direct. They derive, in large measure, from the strategic position of the Middle East in relation to global security and the international order. It is significant that the very term "Middle East" (or its predecessor "Near East") does not refer to characteristics internal to the area, but arose out of the relations to forces which lie beyond its borders, to external centers of power. In a sense, "Middle East" is not a geographic term at all. Its borders are not set so much by natural features as by problems of international relations. It is a political and diplomatic term reflecting the constant interplay between the great powers in Africa, Asia, and Europe and the area which forms the junction between them. By that definition, there is no doubt that the eastern part of the Arab world lies near the center of the world security problem.

Obviously their strategic location makes the communication facilities of the Middle East an international concern. With the Mediterranean Sea, the Red Sea and the Persian Gulf penetrating the Eurasian land mass, the land, air and sea routes linking the hemispheres cross here. The Middle East has thus long been the vestibule of east-west communication, particularly for any power having interests or bearing responsibilities in Asia and Africa.

Technical developments are affecting the nature and importance of transportation facilities. Long-range, high-flying planes in the future may not need the landing and servicing facilities of Arab world airports to maintain intercontinental connections. Supertankers are already by-passing the Suez Canal for the route around Africa. Yet for the present and immediate future, the Middle East will continue to play an important role in military and commercial world communications. Access to them in peace and in war remains essential for the development and security of many nations.

The Arab lands occupy a special position in the Middle Eastern corridor. The decolonization of Africa has lessened the accessibility of the alternate trans-African route used during World War II. Although the northern tier states of Turkey, Iran, and Pakistan are politically more cooperative with the West, their geographical position is peripheral to the main route of Middle Eastern communications, which still lie chiefly within Arab lands: the Suez Canal, the air routes from Cairo and Beirut to the Persian Gulf and across Libya and the Sudan to East Africa and the Indian Ocean. Access to these routes under reasonable conditions, unimpeded passage of the Suez Canal, and rights of overflight form an American interest at the present time so basic that any continued and serious threat would engender a strong response.

Of comparable importance is the interest in access to the petroleum supplies of the area. Middle Eastern petroleum is a principal source of power for the Western European economy (60 per cent of whose oil imports come from this area) and a basic resource in global defense. Although the development of atomic power and of alternate sources of oil are reducing the importance of Middle Eastern petroleum, for the present it is an important interest of the free world. This interest is not to be confused with the commercial and concessionary arrangements under which Middle East petroleum is currently exploited. What is vital to Western security is that oil be available on reasonable terms, whether produced under present arrangements, under some revision of existing concessionary agreements, or by nationalized oil companies. It is the *availability,* not the concessionary arrangements, which is the interest. Like communications, the interest in petroleum is so vital that a serious threat to it would bring a strong American reaction.

These interests are specific, basic, vital. They heighten other interests whose existence is a concomitant to the Western position in the area. The first and foremost is that the Middle East, or any vital part of it, shall not be occupied or controlled by a foreign power hostile to the United States and the free world. Such a power could either deny oil and passage to the West, or use access to them as diplomatic blackmail to force changes in Western policy. Here also the global aspects of American policy are pertinent. The falling of Middle Eastern nations into hostile hands would have a shattering political effect on the Western world. Strategically, it could mean a major shift in the balance of power.

At present, the only serious threat of such hostile control comes from the Communist world—specifically the U.S.S.R. While the Soviet satellites have played a role in the Middle East in supporting Russian policies, they are now becoming more independent of Soviet control. In any case, they are not capable on their own of imperiling the Western position. Nor has Communist China yet demonstrated that it can challenge or replace the Soviet Union or be a serious threat to the West in the area. Thus the problem is to contain Soviet influence. This does not mean the eradication of all Soviet influence or presence in the area—desirable as many Westerners would consider that to be—for the U.S.S.R. has become an important fact of life in the Arab world. The question is not whether the history of Soviet penetration can now be undone and the Russian presence and influence removed, but whether these can be contained short of the point where their influence in Arab lands dominates Arab policy to the detriment of the interests of the free world.

Despite the growth and variety of Soviet activity in the area, a Russian takeover of any Middle Eastern state has not yet occurred. It is noteworthy that after a decade of Soviet influence no Arab country can properly be called a Soviet satellite, nor has any permitted a Communist party to exist, or irrevocably lost a significant measure of its freedom of action to the Soviets. Despite Arab preoccupation with "neocolonialism" and the remnants of British colonialism, it is not from the West that the threat to independence comes. Communist imperialism, expressed either through control of radical indigenous forces or by overwhelming economic and political pressure, is the shadow which hangs over independence of the Arab world.

At the beginning of the postwar period, it was the defense of the Middle East which formed the focus of American interest. In what sense is Middle East defense an American interest today? From one viewpoint it is still the most basic, since the defense capability would be the final response to any attempt at a Soviet takeover. But the policies needed to serve the interest are no longer the same as a decade ago. Military weaponry and strategy have so changed that bases on Middle Eastern soil are not essential for effective military action on the part of the United States. Moreover, despite the large amount of military assistance given to those Middle Eastern governments willing to receive it (Iran, Turkey, and peripherally, Pakistan and Greece, with smaller amounts going to Jordan and Saudi Arabia), the capability of indigenous forces to defend their frontiers or to contribute significantly to American defense of the area must now be questioned. In the Arab world there is no desire to collaborate on defense with the United States unless that collaboration includes defense against Israel. Thus the instruments for defense of American interests have moved largely outside Arab borders to adjacent seas where the Sixth Fleet is stationed and to American defense installations in other parts of the world.

In protecting these interests, there are certain conditions within the Middle East which must concern the United States. The first is the independence of Middle Eastern governments. No matter what the form of a government or its general characteristics—whether traditional or revolutionary, pro-West or pro-East—the loss of independence by any Arab country to a foreign power (specifically to a Communist power) could seriously imperil American interests.

Reasonable tranquility within the area also bears upon American interests. The attack of one Middle East state on another state where the United States has a direct interest (such as petroleum in Saudi Arabia, or the Suez Canal in the U.A.R.) would evoke grave American concern. The threat could arise either by the conquest of one country by another with the object of cutting off Western access, or by the emergence in a particular country of a regime which would follow a similar policy. The latter possibility is more difficult to meet than overt military action, since it involves the internal acts of a sovereign state. Amalgamation of two Arab countries, either by consent or conquest, would not necessarily threaten vital American interests, unless the result were a denial of access to oil and communications on reasonable terms. Moreover, intra-area quarrels invite outside interference (as witness Soviet threats at the time of the Israeli-Anglo-French attack on the U.A.R. in 1956 and the Soviet position in the 1967 Arab-Israel confrontation) with the result that Arab independence might be compromised irrevocably or the United States forced into a confrontation with the U.S.S.R. Thus, although the United States cannot enforce tranquility, it does have a strong stake in it.

The general economic and social progress of the Arab world, while much to be desired, is not, in strict definition, an American interest; but insofar as it is connected with conditions affecting American interests it becomes an American concern. And that connection is indeed intimate. Both the stability of individual governments and the tranquility of the area are affected by the intensifying struggle to achieve the transformation of Arab life into a modern, progressive, and more equalitarian pattern. Every

Arab government faces, in some form, a rising tide of popular expectation for change and betterment. In more advanced countries (the U.A.R., Syria, Jordan, Iraq, and lately Kuwait), this pressure is identified with the emerging middle class, the swelling student body, the growth of labor organizations, and the awakening of the rural population to their plight. In more traditional societies (Saudi Arabia, Libya, Yemen and the sheikhdoms of the Arabian Peninsula), the pressure comes from a limited group of technicians and intellectual elite who are in contact with the modern world through travel, education, and involvement in Western enterprises. But regardless of extent or intensity, the demands for and belief in the possibility of reconstructing society is a pressure to which no Arab government can be indifferent. In no country is there as yet a capacity for widespread and popularly organized social movements, yet social and economic discontent provides a tool for political ambitions, as the revolutions in Egypt, Syria, and Iraq so clearly showed.

The pressure for change and the movements it produces are beyond the possibility of control by any external force. The United States cannot be indifferent to this pressure since the instability it creates has an impact on American interests. In principle, the United States stands for change and progress in the Arab world, but its stance is affected by two factors. One is that however desirable change may be, the forces of destruction frequently outrun those of construction. It would not be difficult to overthrow the existing traditional governments in many countries since the tinder of social discontent has long been smouldering. The difficulty is that after the overthrow there may be no effective force, organization or personnel to build a new and stable order. The effect of revolution might well be chaos and economic retrogression rather than constructive growth—a condition which has threatened Syria and Iraq. Especially in a country where there is a major American interest, the United States will consequently tend to shore up an existing regime rather than subject its interests to the vagaries and uncertainties of revolutionary change.

The second factor conditioning the American attitude toward

regional tranquility is, again, that violent change, political instability, and national rivalries run the risk of inviting outside
forces. This is to say that for the short run, relative quiet may
serve American interests better than radical change, although in
the long run it seems probable that radical change in some form
must take place.

Other Concerns

There are two other aspects of relations with the Arab world
that many would consider as American interests. One is the unwavering support of Israel. That country's more dedicated supporters in the United States argue that Israel, as the only democratic society in the area, is an example of progress and development which the Arab states themselves need. In their eyes,
Israel's continued growth is thus a vital American interest. Taken
to the extreme—as it frequently is during domestic political
campaigns—this argument may lead to the proposition that
Israel should be the cornerstone and chosen instrument of
American policy in the dealing with Arab states.

The democratic nature and vigorous development of Israel
can be fully and gratefully recognized, but this does not make
support of Israel an interest of the United States comparable
to those already mentioned, except as its independence is involved. Indeed, for such vital interests, the American connection
with Israel is a liability, not an asset. Those who hold that
American support for Israel is the sole cause for American
difficulties in the Arab world are wrong. Given the character
of the postwar Middle East, the American place in the Western
alliance, and conflicting American-Arab attitudes toward the
cold-war struggle, the United States would have its problems in
the Arab world, even were there no Israel. But Israel is the
most constant, ubiquitous, and deeply emotional cause in the
Arab world. It affects the relations of every Arab state with the
United States, especially at times of crisis. Under the pressure
of immediate interests, such as the production of petroleum or
the securing of economic assistance, an Arab government may

keep its resentment of United States support for Israel in the background—as was true in Egypt between 1961 and 1964. But once the issue becomes active, the basic weakness of the American position in Arab eyes is revealed—as the rapid severing of many Arab-American diplomatic relations during the 1967 Arab-Israel conflict so clearly showed. Of all the Arab disputes which threaten area tranquility and circumscribe the ability of the United States to maintain a constructive relation with Arab countries, the Arab-Israel impasse is the most threatening.

In the context of American foreign policy, Israel thus needs to be viewed as a problem, rather than as an interest. Together with many other countries, the United States is committed to Israel's existence, as based upon, and within the framework of, the actions of the United Nations. The commitment to Israel's continuation as an independent state includes a concern for the conditions which will make this possible and is no different in kind (although it frequently is in degree) from the general American concern for the independence of all Middle Eastern countries, particularly against external military threat.

In practice, however, the concern for Israeli independence differs from that for Arab independence because of internal factors in the United States. Not only do sections of the American public have a personal interest in and connection with Israel, but politicians find in them a source of votes and influence. Consequently, Congress and the State Department are always under pressure to give special consideration to Israel's well-being, even though this may not be in the American interest, as the term is used in this study. By lobbies, campaign contributions and organizations of Americans, proponents of Israel mount a "special pleading" for their cause that no other Middle Eastern state can match. The resulting situation is not unlike that at the end of the nineteenth century, when a large Irish immigrant population devoted to Irish independence constantly injected the "Irish question" into American politics, especially in large Eastern cities.

In these circumstances it has been difficult to maintain steadfastly the limited nature of American commitments to Israel.

The commitments have been set forth in various official policy statements, yet policy-makers are always under pressure to increase them. It is argued that the American commitment to the existence of Israel logically implies a commitment to furnish the means of safeguarding that existence—arms, a special security treaty, joint defense planning, pressure on hostile Arab countries through withdrawal of aid to them—despite the fact that such actions could seriously imperil American interests in the Arab world.

It is at this point that the United States connection with Israel most nearly approaches the status of an "interest." The interest is not one in Israel per se, but in the effects of the Arab-Israel dispute on the stability and tranquility of the area. The breakdown of the 1956 unstable cease-fire endangered continued access to petroleum, increased the immediate prestige of the Soviet Union among the Arabs, and could force revolutionary (and probably chaotic) changes in Arab countries where the United States has special concerns. The American interest thus lies in defusing the Arab-Israel time bomb, not in supporting Israel under every circumstance. This is not to say that the United States will abandon its present commitments to Israel although it may not fulfill them to the measure Israel expects. It does say that these commitments are secondary to vital American interests and thus cannot be allowed to dictate American policy toward the Arab world. A chief element of that policy must be to contain and, wherever possible, reduce the potential of Arab-Israel conflict; and it can lead the United States to pursue courses opposed by Israel as well as by parts of the Arab world. Such questions as the settlement of the refugees, the rectification of Israel-Arab borders, the Arab boycott, and the Arab-Israel arms race must be faced from the viewpoint of American interests, not as Israeli interests.

Another aspect of relations with the Arab world which some in the United States would consider a vital interest is the support and furtherance of democratic government and the free-enterprise economic system. Policies which give support to various military or "strong-man" regimes, with which are often associated some form of state-controlled economy ("Arab socialism" is the current pattern), are attacked as contrary to American aspirations, destructive of American influence, and aiding and abetting the growth of Soviet influence in the area.

Obviously, democracy and free enterprise are good things in American eyes, and their success in the Middle East and Arab world might well benefit both the people of the area and Western interests there. But any realistic view of the situation makes it clear that it would be impossible to conduct a foreign policy in which the fostering of democratic institutions and a free-enterprise economy is rated equal in importance with the strategic interests previously enumerated. For one thing, no Arab country combines both democratic institutions and a free economy in a form which meets the American ideal. Lebanon has a democratic government, but its free enterprise is so uninhibited that it stands far to the right of what many Americans consider desirable in the modern world. Saudi Arabia and Jordan have free enterprise, but are politically undemocratic. Iraq, Syria, and the U.A.R. have adopted various stages of state economic control, turning their backs on the democratic institutions which were the political façade of prerevolutionary days. In fact, no country in the Arab world either fits the American prescription for democracy and free enterprise or shows much likelihood of doing so in the next few decades. Rigorously applied, a policy of promoting democracy and free enterprise as basic American interests would impede the U.S. relations with all Arab states.

Moreover, neither political democracy nor free enterprise are preconditions for the protection of American interests. The question of petroleum is not the system under which it is produced, but its availability. An absolutist government dedicated to a state-directed economy can supply oil to the West as well as a democratic government of free enterprise. Indeed, with its centralization of power and economic planning, it might be easier to deal with an absolutist government than with some of the Middle East's unstable "democracies." The availability of the Suez Canal for world transport does not lie in the form of Egyptian government and economics, but in Egyptian policy, which is based on that country's interest in utilizing one of its major sources of hard currency. The American concern for independence in the Arab world is not limited to those states which are most sympathetic to the Western political and economic pattern; it applies (under the conditions outlined above) to all states. Whatever characteristics the present U.A.R. may have, its loss of independence to the U.S.S.R. would seriously endanger American interests in the Middle East. Clearly, the interests of the United States exist in an area where democratic and free enterprise are notably lacking and unlikely to develop in the near future.

In addition, the United States does not have the capability of forcing democracy and free enterprise on the Arab world. The absence of these Western institutions is not due primarily to the whim of a leader or his regime; it is rooted in the nature of Arab society, the inheritance of the past, the pressure to catch up with the modern world after centuries of underdevelopment, and the unsatisfactory experience of Arab states with imported Western systems. American foreign policy cannot change these factors; to attempt to do so by making the change a prime American interest is only to limit the ability of the United States to protect and further its truly strategic interests.

This is not to say that the United States has no concern for the forms of government and economics in the Arab world. Like the Soviet Union, many Americans would prefer to see developing countries adopt a pattern similar to their own. Yet, as the Soviet experience has demonstrated, failure to effect this does not necessarily close the door to working relations with Arab governments in their present form. Indeed, if any influence for political and economic development is to be wielded, it can only be done through maintaining such relations. Those who call for indefinite suspension of aid to the U.A.R. because it is a "socialist dictatorship" are asking the United States not only to abandon those American interests in which the U.A.R. has an important role, but also to close the door to any possibility of influencing the development of its government and society.

Such influence will not come as a result of direct pressure—a precondition to undertaking aid projects or to political relations —but through the continued association of Americans and Arabs in projects of mutual interest. Political suspicions are one cause for the Arab retreat from Western institutions; the better and more consistent are Arab relations with the United States, the better the setting for confidence in the character of the American system. Furthermore, the efficiency with which foreign aid and private business operate in Arab lands is a factor in the Arab judgment of the Western economic system. Here the West is in direct competition with the Soviets; the result will depend not so much upon ideological argument as upon demonstration.

There is one other aspect of Arab affairs which is of growing concern to the United States, namely, the policies and activities of some governments of the area toward critical international situations, such as the Congo, Cyprus, and Viet Nam. Their opposition and criticism has not affected the basic security of the United States. Nor do they deal with issues or conditions for which the United States can undertake direct commitment to act in the Middle East. Yet the international policies and actions of Middle Eastern governments may affect U.S. interests in other parts of the world and stand in opposition to international efforts towards the resolution of dangerous disputes. They may also inhibit the ability of the U.S. government to sustain a constructive and consistent policy toward Middle Eastern countries.

Non-Arab states of the Middle East (Turkey, Iran, Pakistan) have defense relations with the West through NATO and CENTO, which reflect their general support of the Western position in many international matters. In recent years, this has been less true of Pakistan, especially in matters relating to Communist China. The Arab states, however, have no such defense connection, having adopted the policy of nonalignment. Many of them at times take the same line as the Communist states, especially on colonial questions. To varying degrees, they identify themselves with the brotherhood of emerging states rather than with the Western powers and often express this by opposing Western policies in international tension spots. The Afro-Asian bloc, the

Bandung group, and the nonaligned fellowship offer them international connections which are replacing their pro-West tradition of prewar days.

Arab attitudes and actions toward critical international situations concern the United States for two reasons. One is that they may encourage and prolong the international problem which the West is seeking to resolve. The supply of arms to the Congo rebels and to the Cyprus government by the U.A.R. did not help moderate strife. Moreover, such acts and the policies from which they spring may affect and infect the nonaligned and Afro-Asian groups. The result is to inhibit the peace-keeping efforts of the United Nations as well as to create difficulties for the United States in its relations with individual emerging states.

The ability of the United States to sustain a steady and constructive policy toward individual Arab states is also affected by their international stance. Whether or not U.A.R. activities in the Congo and Cyprus were actually effective (and they probably were not), they had a deep impact on congressional, State Department, and presidential attitudes. When the U.A.R. was supplying arms clandestinely to the Congo rebels while the United States was supporting U.N. efforts to end the struggle, it was extremely difficult to obtain a favorable hearing for the economic needs of the U.A.R. The reason is not that policy-makers put a direct political price on economic aid programs. Rather, the recipient country, by its own acts, created a public image which made it appear as indifferent, or opposed to American and international efforts for tranquility and peace. This is the more true when there is no apparent Arab national interest at stake. Certainly, Arab security was not imperilled by the outcome of the Congo situation; Algerian and U.A.R. support for the rebels was not comprehensible as a vital Arab interest. In the circumstances, it is often impossible for American policy makers to obtain the public and legislative support needed to continue a mutually useful relation with the Arab country involved.

Important as the American concern for Arab international action is, it has been exaggerated in many instances. Only a few of the Arab states—chiefly Algeria and the U.A.R.—have been active in international disputes beyond the borders of the Middle East. Their ability either to affect the situation directly or to alter the climate of opinion in the nonaligned world is much less than both they and the United States frequently assume. Irresponsible speeches and actions are annoying, but they rarely pose a threat to basic American action. The United States cannot afford the mistake of dignifying such activities by attaching major importance to them in framing a foreign policy for the protection of its own interests.

Chapter III

New Forces in the Arab World

The Arab world, in which the United States has developed a new role, is itself new in many significant ways. To be sure, the traditional features of Arab life and politics have not ceased to be important; not only do they continue as basic forces, but they have taken on renewed significance as the inhibiting controls of the colonial period have ended. Yet the character of the new Arab world with which American foreign policy must deal is found not so much in its traditional patterns as in the social and political changes which have taken place in recent decades.

One of the temptations of area specialization (whether in universities or government agencies) is to seek the key to problems of the region in some "unique" factor such as culture, social organization, religion, or history. The first question often asked is: "Why do the Arabs act like this?" as though there must be a specific *Arab* explanation for the situation. But this should not be the first question; political actions and reactions are initially to be understood in the light of general challenge and response. Only when these have been carefully investigated can the significance of an "Arab" factor be determined. Arabs, Africans, Asians, Europeans, and Americans tend to react in similar ways under similar circumstances of national interest or political and social development. This commonality of reaction is the first clue to the changes which are reshaping the postwar Arab world and with which other states must now deal.

Sovereignty and its Effects

The most ubiquitous and influential of these changes is the emergence of the Arab world into political sovereignty. A century and a half ago, when the West first began its penetration of the Middle East, the area was principally incorporated in two individual, sovereign states: Persia and the Ottoman Empire. For the most part, Arab lands were formally under Turkish rule, although the Arabian peninsula had a number of traditional sheikhdoms, emirates, and imamates which were only distantly or spasmodically controlled by the Ottomans. Turkish control shrank in the following decades as the Western powers became the *de facto* rulers of the region. By the beginning of World War II Saudi Arabia had emerged as an independent Arab state, while Egypt and Iraq were technically sovereign although Great Britain exercised a measure of control over them. Some of the smaller political entities in Arabia retained their historic independence (as Yemen), but many had entered into treaty relations which gave Great Britain a favored position. The rest of the area was a tissue of colonies, mandates, protectorates, and spheres of influence under French and British control. In contrast, there are today eight sovereign Arab states from the borders of Egypt to the Indian Ocean; foreign control is confined to the periphery of the Arabian peninsula, and even there it is rapidly on the wane. For the first time in many centuries, the Arab world is composed of fully independent, self-determining, sovereign states.

Some will cavil at the use of "sovereign" for any state in the modern world, especially the smaller and weaker ones. Obviously, in the fullest sense of the word no state can be sovereign today in that it can do what it wants, as it wants, and when it wants. The destiny of the Arab world, like the destiny of the United States, is so bound to the complexities of international life that its freedom of action is curtailed continuously—a fact to which Arab nationalists have not yet fully adjusted. Yet there is a vast difference between being a colony, mandate, sphere of influence, or object of a treaty of special privilege and being an independent state. The sovereign Arab states are all members of the United Nations, with a direct voice in its proceedings. They maintain their own diplomatic missions abroad, freely negotiate with other states, and have the authority to determine their own affairs —both internal and external—without seeking the permission of some other government. In this sense, they are as sovereign as the United States or any other great power.

The fact of sovereignty has profoundly influenced Arab affairs. For one thing, it has diminished and altered the instruments by which the great powers can protect their interests in the Arab world. With independence, the occupying garrisons are gone, the foreign advisers in government ministries have departed, the treaties of special privilege have been repudiated. National interests of foreign states must now be dealt with through the ordinary give-and-take of diplomacy between equally sovereign states. It is the ambassador, not the high commissioner, foreign ministry adviser or commander of the occupying garrison who must do business with an Arab government; and in doing business he must rely more on the instruments of diplomacy—dialogue and negotiation—than on a special or privileged position.

It has not been easy for the Western world (especially the former colonial powers) to come to terms with this fact. While the sovereign status of Arab states is internationally recognized, it has not always been psychologically accepted. There still are those who feel that some residue of Western control does, or should, exist and that this can be the basis for Western policy in the region. Hence, the strong British and French reaction to Egypt's nationalization of the Suez Canal in 1956, although nationalization (with adequate compensation) of a legally native corporation is not an unusual practice among Western sovereign states themselves. Those who have maintained that the West (or more directly the United States) should "force the Arabs to make peace with Israel" likewise assume the need for Western control, but the assumption is no longer tenable.

The results of the transit from dependence to sovereignty have affected the international attitudes of Arab governments. If the West has had difficulty in clearing from its mind the memories of past dominance, Arabs have had equal difficulty in exorcising their suspicions that every Western policy is aimed at limiting their independence. Economic, cultural, or political proposals put forward by the West are frequently viewed with much more suspicion than those coming from the non-Western world—the natural, if unfortunate, reaction of newly won sovereignty to dealings with past colonial powers. Recent Arab (especially U.A.R.) attitudes toward Great Britain are a case in point. Coincident with the outbreak of trouble in Cyprus at the end of 1963, British assistance was requested by the newly independent states of Uganda, Kenya, and Tanganyika to cope with mutinies in their armed forces. The result was an increase in, or return of, British troops to these former colonial areas. While this move was under way, the British Prime Minister made an unpremeditated statement in Ottawa concerning current American difficulties in the Panama Canal Zone. When asked about his government's attitude, he said that the dispute was not Britain's concern, and he wished that the United States had taken a similar attitude at the time of the Suez Canal problem. The immediate reaction in some Arab countries was that Britain was covertly using the disarray in East Africa and the Middle East to regain a military foothold in the area and begin a "return to colonialism." The United States has experienced, and must continue to expect, similar irrational misinterpretations of its motives and policies, born out of the suspicions and pride of newly achieved sovereignty.

Sovereign status affects not only the attitude of Arab governments toward other nations, but also the attitude of citizens toward their own nation. When national destiny was under some measure of foreign control, failures in economic, political and social progress could always be blamed on "imperialism," which could not be expected to give priority to native development over imperial interest. Although the colonial record of France and Great Britain in the Arab world is much better than Arab nationalists admit, it did not keep pace with the growing demands for economic, educational, social and political progress, and thus appeared to be the major obstacle to the achievement of modernity. Now that the foreigner has departed and responsibility is in the hands of "our" national leaders, there is a popular expectation that everything will be put right. Although national leaders may still try to blame their country's internal problems on the "neocolonialists," their public is not so easily misled. Having been told for at least a generation that the departure of the foreigner was the precondition for national progress, the masses gradually tend to hold their own leaders responsible for current failures.

To this attitude is coupled a change in the status of the individual in relation to his government. Under colonialism the local inhabitant was a "subject," his destiny either directly or more distantly controlled by a power to which he had no effective relation. In the sovereign state, subjects disappear to be replaced by citizens who (at least in theory) have the right and duty of direct involvement in their national affairs. When President Nasser addresses the Egyptian masses as "muwatinun"—"citizens"—he is invoking a new status for the common man of the Nile Valley. To be sure, few Arab states thus far have provided adequately for the participation of their citizenry in the tasks of nationhood. Too often it may appear that the passage to independence is only the substitution of an indigenous master for a foreign one. Yet it is never simply a substitution. The new masters face a growing, if inchoate, demand for some form of participation by citizens in the tasks and opportunities of their new nation. To develop political and social institutions which provide this participation is the major challenge of sovereignty, and failure to meet it in reasonable measure is its major peril.

There are other new responsibilities and problems which independence has brought. Not only has the full burden of traditional government services been placed upon the new states, but they are being called to provide public health, education, technical training, wage and price controls, village improvement, agricultural development, labor organization, expanded public transportation—to name only a few of the services necessary to a modern, or modernizing society. Yet for such tasks they often lack both experience and trained personnel. It takes time to develop both, but popular pressure and nationalist expectation are such that a too deliberate pace, however realistic, cannot meet the need. The dilemma is illustrated by two attitudes toward the state-operated economic system of the U.A.R.—"Arab socialism." One senior policy-planner in Cairo said, "The peasant has been so long deprived of even minimal decency that he cannot be made to wait much longer. In spite of everything, we must push on even more rapidly." In contrast, an Arab diplomat said that he had lost his faith in Arab socialism, not because he disagreed with its theory, but because "when you take an already over-burdened and inefficient civil service, then add to it the huge responsibility of running an industrial system, the result can only be a complete breakdown."

Such effects of sovereignty on the Arab states are a factor conditioning the shape and conduct of their international relations, and accounting for much of the instability which runs counter to the international interests in peace and orderly progress. These effects may lead government to undertake programs of development in which national resources are not used efficiently. At times they cause an unpredictable quality in many Arab policies, which makes it difficult for foreign aid programs to contribute effectively toward social and economic development. They form a focus of nationalistic feeling which in Arab eyes may take precedence over the requirements of their own foreign policy—sometimes seriously disturbing relations with another country at the very time urgent demands are being made on it for economic assistance. The tug of these contrary forces has been a continuous factor in U.A.R.—U.S. relations. The accelerating pace of national development leads to repeated and urgent requests for American assistance. Yet the U.A.R. government has seemed unable to comprehend that some of its foreign policies make such assistance extremely difficult to defend to the American Congress and public who in the end must pay the bill.

In larger terms, the impact of sovereignty on the outlook and status of the Arab populace is such that no foreign policy toward the Arab world can be aimed solely at the Arab governments of the moment on the theory that the masses do not count. However unpalatable or difficult an Arab leader's policies may be, the needs, aspirations, and future role of the new citizenry cannot be neglected on that account. They may be holding the key to the future, and a policy toward their country must be concerned with a relationship to their presence as well as to the government currently in power. American food programs may temporarily support a government or leader who causes the United States problems, but the food also contributes to the welfare of the common people and to some degree identifies the United States with their problems. Both factors must be taken into account in formulating a policy on food aid.

Nonalignment

Another new force in the Arab world is nonalignment or neutralism, adopted as a basic foreign policy by all the sovereign Arab states. The precise character, detailed policies, and results of nonalignment vary widely between them, as the discussions at Arab League meetings and at the 1964 Conference of Nonaligned Countries in Cairo revealed. In the more radical states (U.A.R., Syria, Iraq), the Soviet connection has been cultivated and exploited both as a counterweight to the West and as a resource for national development and international position. Here the Soviets have mounted large aid programs, supplied arms, encouraged the governments in dispute with the West, and elicited some significant support in government circles. In contrast, the more traditional states (Jordan, Saudi Arabia) have either refused to accept diplomatic relations with the Soviet Union or have thus far dealt cautiously with it in terms which do not alter their established Western connections. In many ways their nonalignment is as pro-Western as the radical states' is pro-Eastern.

Despite such differences, nonalignment (the refusal to make any formal alliance with a great power) is the basic international stance of the Arab world, standing in marked contrast to the political presuppositions of the earlier era. Then the assumption underlying Western policies, especially British, was that the community of interests between the Arab world and the West could be cultivated into a permanent partnership. Arab nationalists of the period largely accepted this premise. While struggling for political freedom from Anglo-French control, they envisioned a continuing major relation with the West after independence, which they considered essential for the economic and political well-being of their countries. This assumption has been repudiated in the adoption of nonalignment. It is not that Arab countries necessarily seek to end their Western connections, for a community of interests still exists. Rather, the connection is not accepted as necessarily a foregone conclusion, and Arab governments feel free to enter into relations with any country and adopt any international policy which they consider to their benefit.

Arab nonalignment was not due directly to the intrusion of the cold war into the Middle East. The extension of the East-West struggle into the area was the *occasion* for the emergence of neutralism, but its *causes* lie beyond the cold war. They are rooted in the inherently anti-Western character of Arab political independence.

Not surprisingly, with the attainment of independence and sovereignty after the Second World War, the Arab world reacted against its experience of foreign control and sought to turn away from political commitments and alignments. They felt no concern for supporting the West in a world power struggle; the only "free world" in which they were vitally interested was their own free world—free from any remnants of Western control which had so long directed their destinies and involved them in two destructive world wars not of their making. Every Western move to secure Arab collaboration in the struggle with the Soviet Union was viewed by Arab nationalists as an occasion (or perhaps an excuse) for reinstating some measure of Western control over their affairs. Moreover, the Western (especially American) identification with the creation and support of Israel made it impossible for the Arab states to join permanently with those they considered the friends of their enemies.

If half of the policy of nonalignment is based on this Arab suspicion of cooperation with Western powers in international affairs, the other half—the Soviet connection—came from the inescapable need of Arab states to maintain some form of partnership with stronger and more advanced societies.

In modern times the Middle East as a whole has needed a European connection to support its economic, technological, and political development. Economically, any given country in the region trades more with outside powers (traditionally European) than with any of its neighbors. Egyptian cotton, Arab oil, Iraqi wheat—all have been dependent upon European markets. Culturally and technologically, the Arab world turns to the universities, educational systems, and training centers of Europe for both the pattern of its own programs and the preparation of its advanced technicians. This dependence still holds despite the noteworthy growth in education and training in Arab countries. The increased tempo of national development under independence makes a technical connection with outside powers more, not less, necessary. Politically, the Arab world, like many emerging regions, can only set its course in relation to and (if possible) with the support of major world powers whose influence is paramount in international affairs.

For these reasons the Arab countries, despite their struggle for independence, never quite came to the point of breaking completely with the dominant Western powers before the war. However much the European occupation curtailed their freedom and wounded their pride, it did make possible a relation with European markets, factories, and foreign offices without which their countries could not flourish. A break could only come if there were some substitute for the historic European connection.

That substitute emerged in the postwar world through the new role and influence of the Soviet Union. With nearly half of Europe in its economic and political control, displaying a technological ability of impressive order, and obviously standing as one of the two great power centers in the world, the Soviet Union was able to offer itself as the "new Europe" to many developing nations. Especially after the death of Stalin, Soviet tactics in the Arab world shifted from reliance on the Communist image and Arab movements supporting it to the image of both the "great power" and the "new Europe." The U.S.S.R. could offer aid and trade, technology and training, and political support for national aspirations, giving the Arab world an alternative to reliance upon Western European powers. Given the inherent anti-Westernism of Arab independence, it was inevitable that some Arab states would open up relations with the Communist world as a counterweight, or an alternative, to the tie with the West.

Thus, nonalignment appeared in the Arab world, built upon forces more basic than the cold war, but given its shape and sustained by the cold-war struggle. Its appearance formed a new factor deeply affecting the foreign policies of all powers toward the Arab world. Nonalignment has limited the degree and kind of cold-war pressure which either side can apply. It has meant that Arab states cannot be counted upon to support the foreign policies either of the West or the East. Arab states generally opposed Soviet policies on resumption of nuclear testing and on reorganizing the United Nations, and most of them have opposed American policy toward Viet Nam. Arab governments have been able at times to put pressure on the Soviet Union and the West by threatening to increase their dealings with the other side. And by their proclaimed nonalignment Arab governments have found a new set of international partners in the Afro-Asian and non-aligned groups, although these partners seldom act in concert.

Although nonalignment has remained the official policy of every Arab state, the significance and implications of this position have constantly altered. When relations between the West and the Soviet Union improve and the concept of the cold war softens, the possibility and utility of playing one side off against the other is lessened. The coherence of a global nonaligned group (to the extent that it ever existed) has steadily weakened, reducing the possibility that any set of nations (as the Arab states) can or will act in concert on that basis. Individual Arab states find that their

national interests and problems (such as the Yemen war) neces-
sitate close relations with one or another of the world powers,
despite their nonaligned status. Yet for all these changes, nonalignment has remained a significant expression of Arab sovereignty in its right to repudiate an unwavering alliance with any
center of world power and freely to choose those international
partners which best serve its own interests.

The New Nationalism

Nonalignment is in part a reflection of the changing character
of nationalism in the Arab world. In many Arab countries nationalism has entered a second stage; it is being conducted by new
leaders, is supported by new popular forces, and faces new problems. Prewar nationalism was largely headed by the traditional
elite—large land owners, urban merchants, and tribal leaders.
The professional classes were sometimes involved, although many
shunned political activity as unworthy of their status. Many of
these leaders received at least part of their education in Europe
and drew from there the political and social ideals they sought
in the struggle for independence. In a sense, it was because they
were so pro-Western that they fought against the political domination of the West, claiming for their countries the forms of
goverment and social institutions they believed to be the secret
of Western power. This was especially true of the rising group
of modern intellectuals who saw in Western liberal institutions
an instrument to curtail the oriental despotism which kept their
societies backward and to create a new order in which they could
play a leading role. The policy of Western powers in introducing
limited forms of constitutional parliamentary life into their
colonies and mandates was welcomed by the liberal nationalists as
a necessary step to independence and modernity.

During this period the masses played a minor role. It was always possible for a nationalist leader to whip up a demonstration
against the French or the British, but it was usually only a
demonstration, not a sustained popular movement. The common
man of the city and countryside had little sense of identification

with his political leaders, and was absorbed in the business of earning a precarious daily living. Waves of nationalist feeling periodically would sweep a country, as in the anti-British Egyptian riots of the 1920s, but the heart of the national movement lay in the upper urban elite which organized and gave continuity to the struggle.

In general, the postwar national movements in Arab lands have taken on new characteristics. One of these is the change of leadership, both in person and in character. The Nahas Pashas and Nuri Saids have been replaced by the Nassers and the Arifs, who are quite different kinds of persons. The older leaders were the products both of Western education and of the Islamic reform movements of the nineteenth century. Nearly all the earlier nationalist leaders in Egypt, for example, had sat at the feet of Mohammed Abdou, the great Muslim scholar of the last century who effectively combined the modernization of Islamic teaching with nationalist aims. In contrast, many of the new national leaders know the West only at second hand, having been trained in local schools heavily tinctured with nationalist feeling. They owe almost no debt to Muslim political thought and seem little influenced by the its concepts. They have been called "new men" in whom the connection with the past (both its Western and politically Islamic orientation) has been replaced by a secular dedication to the tasks of modernization.

Such "new men" are not everywhere in control of Arab national movements, but the tide of the future seems to be flowing in their direction. One of their advantages is that they represent a new level of society. The earlier leaders were of the traditional elite, who lacked close connection with the common man and had an inherited position to maintain. In a sense their nationalism was the revolt of one elite class against another—a native elite against an imposed foreign one. But the new nationalism is increasingly a revolt of middle and lower classes against the traditional native elite. Leaders like Nasser, Kassem, and the Arif brothers came from middle-class backgrounds and are more typically "common man" than those they displaced. Even in nonrevolutionary Arab countries this challenge to traditional elite leadership is beginning to appear. In Kuwait the ruling family and its coterie of supporters are being pressed by those who a decade ago were content to sit in the shadow of the rich merchants and leading sheikhs. This so embarrassed some members of the National Assembly that they resigned rather than subject themselves to parliamentary questioning and criticism from those who had been their families' clients only a few years before.

Behind such new leaders (actual and potential) stand elements of a new following. Years of national struggle, even though sporadic, introduced the common man into his first experience of political participation and national identification. Independence, with its slogans of freedom, has sharpened his interest and deepened his identity with his country. Mass communications, especially the transistor radio, have brought the propaganda of the surrounding world, as well as of his own government, to his coffee house and home. The rapid growth of national education has swelled the ranks of the literate and produced a restless student class, rooted in the middle and lower levels of society yet hungry for the prerogatives of social position, salary, and political significance. In Jordan the massive influx of dispossessed Palestinians with their political awareness and their special sense of grievance eroded the power of the East Bank tribal society on which the stability of the government rested. In Arabia the burgeoning oil industry has created a growing group of entrepreneurs and technicians who are restive under the limited opportunities and slow progress of their traditional society. At a lower level, the awakening of the fellahin to their plight and their dawning consciousness that something can be done about it also creates a restlessness which can build up a potential for popular political action when the leader and the occasion come forward.

As the middle and lower classes in an Arab country awaken to political consciousness and struggle against their own elite, a new element of instability is introduced which makes it difficult to mount a consistent foreign policy toward that country. The depth and ubiquity of national feeling against foreign pressure inhibits forms of action which foreign powers had been able to use in the past. A successful British administrator in the Middle East said that his colonial policy was based on "controlling the 300 people who control the country." Although the power centers in many Arab lands are still small, their roots grow much deeper into the popular life of the country, and they cannot be controlled in the sense that the "300" once were.

Both the leaders and their followers in the postwar chapter of Arab history move in a new dimension of political consciousness—"Arab nationalism." This term stands in contrast to the separate "nationalisms" of Arab states which mainly characterized the struggles of Arab peoples for independence during the inter-war period. When the Arab revolt of the First World War failed to produce a single Arab state (embracing what is now Israel, Jordan, Syria, the Hejaz, and Iraq) its remnants were fragmented into local nationalist movements. The center of attention became the struggle of populations in the newly created states against the European power which immediately controlled them. There was little contact between or coordination with the national struggles of neighboring countries; Syria, Iraq, Lebanon, Egypt, each went its own way and fought its own battles for freedom. Even though the Arab countries which were created under the mandate system had a degree of political and geographic artificiality, the inter-war decades of inculcated local patriotism and national struggle created a sense of national identity which has persisted ever since.

After the Second World War there was growing discontent among Arab leaders with the "Balkanization" of the eastern Arab world. Great Britain encouraged the first moves toward regional organization, which culminated in the formation of the League of Arab States in 1945. The discussion of regional pacts in the early days of the United Nations further stimulated Arab concern. In particular the creation of Israel posed a general problem which drew the Arab states together in a brotherhood of hostility against a situation which no single state could challenge by itself. Ever since, Israel has remained the most constant ingredient in the Arab longing to achieve some larger degree of unity.

Accompanying and stimulated by these developments was a new passion for the "Arab Nation"—a concept overarching existing Arab states and envisioned as the true and most legitimate expression of the political life of the Arab peoples. The separate nationalisms of Arab countries were attacked in theory as being the heritage of colonialism, introduced and cultivated by the imperial powers as instruments to divide and control the awakening Arab world. Thus a Syrian diplomat told an American audience that he was ashamed to appear before them as a representative of Syria. "I should stand here", he said, "as a representative of the great Arab Nation." Some of the Arab states have expressed the same feeling in their constitutions, where it is stated that the country is a part of the Arab Nation, thus suggesting an ultimate loyalty higher than local patriotism.

As a psychological fact, the feeling of Arab nationalism is almost ubiquitous in most of the eastern Arab states. It is particularly the devotion of the student generation, as any discussion with them on Arab politics immediately reveals. The trouble is that the reality of political unity has been unable to keep pace with the growth of psychological loyalty to it. The union of Syria and Egypt in 1958 to form the United Arab Republic was hailed with widespread enthusiasm as the harbinger of growing political unity. The collapse of that union in 1961 and the dismal failure to revive it (with the addition of Iraq) in 1963 seemed to write finis to any hope of effective political unity in the near future. Intra-Arab quarrels, even to the point of using Arab troops in Yemen to slaughter other Arabs, were seemingly irrefutable arguments that while Arabs could talk about the Arab Nation and feel deeply the claims of Arab nationalism, they could do little about it in the practical sphere of political organization. The frustration of this dichotomy of desire and possibility has created a malaise which deeply infects Arab affairs. The separate nationalisms of individual countries are an overwhelming factor in all the area's problems, yet in accepting this inevitable situation, Arab nationalists live with an accusing conscience and a wistful longing for the unrealized, which leaves them baffled and difficult to deal with.

Intra-Arab Differences

Another new force in the Arab world is the heightening of rivalry and strife among the Arabs themselves. In recent years there has been an increasing number of conflicts between Arab countries, some coming to the verge of armed confrontation. Jordan has periodically felt its existence threatened by Egypt and Syria. In 1959 the U.A.R. and Iraq were at swords' points. The separation of Syria from Egypt in 1961 led to a cold war between the two countries, although both governments were dedicated to revolution and followed the same general social philosophy. Under Kassem, Iraq moved in 1961 to enforce its claims on Kuwait, only to be checkmated by British action, followed by the dispatch of an Arab token force of Egyptians and Saudi Arabians under the Arab League. After the Yemen coup d'état of 1962 Saudi Arabi and the U.A.R. continued to move from crisis to crisis over the affair. Enveloping such overt actions has been a fog of radio propaganda and press attacks which would convince any listener that no Arab state trusts or approves its neighbors.

This is indeed a new condition in the modern Arab world. From the Egyptian campaigns in Syria and Arabia in the middle of the nineteenth century to the end of the Second World War, such alarms and excursions were almost unknown. Only the brief Saudi-Yemen war of 1934 troubled the peace of the area. The explanation is simple: the Arab world was then under the control of one or two foreign powers who held the check-rein on local ambitions and disputes. Even in its latter-day weakness the Turkish Empire could exercise some control over Arab lands. When France and Great Britain became the dominant powers in the Arab world, only a dispute between them could open the possibility of a dispute between the colonies and mandates they controlled. When Britain's right hand was in Cairo, and her left hand in Amman, a conflict between Egypt and Transjordan was impossible. The Arab world was peaceful because it had a large degree of centralized, if imposed, political control.

With postwar independence that control vanished. It is the nature of the sovereign state to seek first its own national interests. With eight sovereign states in the eastern Arab world, whose interests are far more diverse than the popular slogans of Arab unity recognize, it was inevitable that there should be differences and tensions between them. For one thing, their forms of government and conditions of society vary widely. They run the gamut from traditional tribalism through agricultural economies to commercial and emerging industrial systems. Their governments range from traditional Arab rule (Kuwait, Saudi Arabia), constitutional monarchy (Jordan), republican democracy (Lebanon), to army-based regimes (Iraq, Syria, U.A.R.). But Arab countries not only live under different systems; they also live in different centuries. Yemen and Abu Dhabi are still medieval. Bahrein and Saudi Arabia have partly entered the twentieth century. Urban life in the U.A.R., Iraq, Syria, and Jordan is modern, but the fellahin lag far behind. Kuwait and Lebanon are enthusiastically of the modern age. These time differences are reflected partly in the role of religion in society. With the exception of Lebanon, all Arab states are Muslim, but Islam does not play the same role in each. In the Arabian peninsula, governments are traditionally Islamic and Sharia law rules the land. The U.A.R. and Syria, in contrast, have become secular in most of their policies, with religious leadership playing only a minor political role. Such differences inevitably lead to differences in economic policies, social developments, and foreign relations.

The national security demands of each state also differ. Throughout history whenever Egypt has been strong and independent it has sought to exercise a measure of control over the gateways to the Valley of the Nile. Saudi Arabia has wished to prevent any rival power from gaining a foothold on the Arabian Peninsula. Both Jordan and Saudi Arabia saw in the overthrow of a traditional ruler in Yemen an infection which might spread to their own countries and threaten their own stability. Lebanon, with its careful balance of minorities as the basis of its democracy, is uncomfortably aware of the encircling Muslim world and the radical movements emanating from it which could destroy this balance.

Postwar sovereignty provided the setting in which, for the first time in the modern world, such differences could become operative. The result was the stress and strain of intra-Arab relations and their growing record of discord and conflict. At times, the record bothers the Arabs themselves. The Arab League has been increasingly concerned with alleviating clashes between its members; the widespread interest in Arab unity, previously noted, is a popular reaction against the divisions of the Arab world and the problems they cause.

Nevertheless, there seems little hope that the tensions between Arab states will diminish in the near future. The dynamics of sovereignty and the pressure of national interests here (as everywhere) continue to operate and create strains between sister states more powerful than the forces drawing them together.

The ephemeral Syrian-Egyptian union of 1958–61 is a warning of how difficult that task will be. Here many of the forces of disunity can be clearly seen—the temptation for a large country to dominate a small one, differences in economic systems and outlook, sharp contrasts in national character. It is apparent that the common "Arabness" of the Syrians and Egyptians was less powerful than their regional and national diversities. If these doomed the union of two countries which had much in common, what hope is there for the amalgamation of eight countries with a far greater range of differences? Local unions between similar and adjacent states may eventually emerge and the Arab League can play a larger role as a clearing house for Arab disputes. But the uniting of the Arab states into a single political unit is at least as distant as is the political unification of Europe.

The tensions and strains among the Arab states are a major problem in defining and conducting foreign policy. Even the concept of an underlying identity of interests which might be the basis for a general Arab policy is rarely valid. Only in their common espousal of nonalignment and their opposition to

Israel do the Arab states agree—and within this agreement there are marked differences of outlook and action. Outside powers, accordingly, find it impossible to sustain a policy toward the "Arab world," for no such world exists in political fact. They may see benefits in expressing support of general Arab aspirations, but specific interests vary from one Arab country to another. This creates the traditional problem of how to defend interests in countries which are in dispute with each other. Thus, American relations with the U.A.R. and the aid program which supported them at times have been resented and attacked by Saudi Arabia and the other nonrevolutionary states of the area. Each accused the United States of supporting its enemies and neglecting its friends. At the same time, the U.A.R. and its fellow radical governments believe that the United States cannot have sustained good relations with them because Western interests in petroleum make American support for the rival traditional camp inevitable.

Moreover, Arab rivalries and conflicts provide the tinder which could be ignited into a major conflagration in the area. The Yemen dispute clearly shows this flammability. Here is a remote and backward part of the Arab world—the Tibet of the area—which no one identified as a threat to anyone's peace. Yet a coup d'état by an unknown army officer in its distant capital of Sana quickly brought about a confrontation between Saudi Arabia, Jordan and the U.A.R., galvanized British reaction in South Arabia, increased Soviet arms and influence in the Arab world, brought the first massive occupation in modern times of one Arab country by another, and involved yet one more United Nations peace-keeping operation, which did not succeed.

Of all the disputes in the area, the Arab-Israel conflict is the most sustained and has the largest potential for escalation. In principle, all Arab governments are committed to unwavering opposition to Israel; no Arab leader can moderate his stand without being attacked by other Arab states, as Bourguiba found in 1965. The issue of Israel unites but it also divides. It is a cause of tension and recrimination within Arab ranks, frustrating and dividing their counsels and providing a ready instrument when one Arab leader wants to attack another. Yet it has been so central to Arab policy and has reached so deeply into the emotions of the masses that a local conflict between Israel and an Arab neighbor can quickly lead to general conflict—as the escalation of Syrian-Israeli clashes led to all-out war in June 1967. The war immediately revived unified Arab action and demonstrated the pressure all Arab leaders are under to sink their differences in the face of an Israeli threat. Feisal quickly proclaimed his readiness to come to terms with Nasser over Yemen, so that Saudi Arabia could give its full resources to the struggle to regain Palestine, while Jordan entered into a mutual defense pact with the U.A.R., although only a few weeks earlier Nasser and Hussein had been bitterly attacking each other. Yet this unity is probably ephemeral; in the aftermath of the disastrous Arab defeat, recriminations as to the causes of and responsibility for Arab failure may once again make the Palestine issue a divisive factor in Arab politics.

In general, area disputes contain a double danger. They may lead to conflicts between the Arab states, which waste their resources, retard their internal development, and may destroy their always tentative political stability. They could also force or tempt some form of foreign involvement which could widen the conflict. Increasingly, the peace of the world has come to rest in such unlikely spots as Cuba, the Congo, Viet Nam, and Yemen, where local disputes may call forth great power support. The Arab world is so strategically located and has been so long enmeshed in world power rivalries that its disarray always has a possible international dimension.

Modernizing the Traditional Middle East

Exacerbating the clash of interests between sovereign states is a political and ideological cold war which is being waged within the Arab world. This is not primarily a facet of the larger global cold war although that struggle at times has been related to it. The Arab cold war is born of the question as to how the traditional societies of the Middle East shall be modernized. On the one hand there are those from Ataturk to Nasser and Ben Bella, who hold that only a revolutionary onslaught on the forms and institutions of the past could produce the desired future. For them traditional Arab life and institutions were corrupt, outmoded beyond recall, and must be replaced by something like Turkish statism or Arab socialism. On the other hand, there are rulers like the King of Jordan or the Emir of Kuwait who believe that progressive movements and liberal institutions can be grafted onto the stock of traditional society so that a gradual evolution to modernity will take place.

Between the two camps there has been periodic rivalry. If the revolutionary leaders are right, and can prove it by success, the traditional rulers ultimately may lose their thrones and possibly their heads. But if the progressive-traditional rulers can demonstrate that an Arab country can pass into the modern world and solve its basic problems without the destructive upheaval of revolution, then it will be the revolutionary leaders who will suffer eclipse. President Nasser admitted this when he said in a public speech: "A failure of the Arab revolution anywhere is a failure everywhere and a failure anywhere is a failure in Egypt."

These contending views of the paths to modernization have not been confined to national leadership. In practically every Arab country there are groups, often strongest among the student class, who opt for the revolutionary view. Their size and political potential varies widely, but they are an ever-present factor in current political life. The struggle is not merely external— between Arab governments pursuing rival paths—but also internal, involving national groups whose activities may threaten the stability of the existing governments. The disarray in Aden and the South Arabian Federation on the eve of independence involved this factor. As an important port city and British naval base, Aden had been intimately in touch both with the outside world and movements in other Arab countries. It has had a significant labor organization which seeks a political role in the passage from colonial status to independence. There is a considerable sentiment in favor of Arab socialism or some other form of radical social change. But Aden not only has its own traditional merchant elite but, under the Federation worked out by the British, was wedded to the tribal areas which surround it. The latter are traditional in the purest sense, and their leaders and people are strongly attached to the age-old ways of tribal life. One of the complaints of the Adeni nationalists has been that while British policy finally came down on the side of independence, it did not offer a choice as to whether Aden was to be independent on its own or had always to go in harness with the "backward" tribal districts. Eventually the British had to hand over independence in 1967 not to the planned Federation, which collapsed, but to a radical nationalist movement, the National Liberation Front. The struggle was indeed a local manifestation of the Arab cold war.

The sharpness of conflict between the revolutionary and traditional camps has varied. After the separation of Syria from Egypt, it rose to new heights since Egyptian leaders interpreted the basic cause of the Syrian withdrawal to be a repudiation of the revolutionary ideals which Egypt had sought to introduce. In one of his first public speeches after the event, President Nasser stated that Egypt's new foreign policy would be based upon the principle of "unity of goals," which meant that the country could work closely only with other revolutionary societies which shared its major objectives. He envisioned a special U.A.R. relationship to Algeria, a new and revolutionary Syria, Iraq and (after the coup d'état of 1962) Yemen. But this attempt to divide the Arab world into opposing camps that scarcely spoke to each other did not succeed. Within two years Egypt found itself isolated from most of its Arab neighbors. It therefore repudiated the sharpened conflict, and in 1963 Nasser announced a new policy of "unity of work," which meant that it would do business with any Arab country undertaking social change and reform—whatever the program it pursued. This brought about a momentary alleviation of the cold war and a restoration of diplomatic relations by the U.A.R. with Saudi Arabia, Jordan, Tunisia, and Morocco. It was followed by three meetings of the Arab chiefs of state, in which some attempt was made to restore

working relations, if not full confidence, between Arab governments. But the thaw did not last. The overthrow of Ben Bella
in Algeria, the attack upon Sukarno's leadership in Indonesia,
and the overthrow of Nkrumah in Ghana were warnings of
possible danger to other revolutionary leaders. The failure of
the Saudi-U.A.R. agreement to disengage in Yemen, signed in
Jiddah in the summer of 1965, again revived the tension. King
Feisal's attempt to form a partnership with other traditional
rulers of the area brought an immediate response from Egypt,
which once again moved toward its policy of full cooperation
only with fellow revolutionary governments. Only the war with
Israel in 1967 brought them together again, at least for the moment.

These forces of sovereignty, nonalignment, nationalism,
regional conflict and cold war are not the only new factors reshaping Arab life. But they are essential features of the postwar
Arab political profile. In determining the American approach
to the Arab world, they are basic considerations which must
not be underrated. Equally necessary is a realistic appraisal
of the available instruments of diplomacy and the ends they are
able to serve, to which we now turn.

Chapter IV

Implements of Foreign Policy

When the United States entered upon its postwar role in the Middle East it had few instruments of special influence in the area. The image of America in Middle Eastern eyes had been set by a century of philanthropic and mission work and by the American oil concessions at the head of the Persian Gulf. Both were conducted under private auspices and seldom claimed or required special protection from the United States government. In those few instances when an American interest was at stake (as access to the petroleum resources released by the collapse of the Turkish Empire), negotiations had been between the United States and the Western powers dominant in the area—not with Middle East governments themselves.

As the various mandated or occupied territories became independent during the interwar period, the United States opened diplomatic relations with them, but this did not lead to close and continuing associations. America's greatest asset in Arab lands was its reputation for disinterested humanitarianism, as embodied in schools, colleges, and hospitals, and its record of noninvolvement in Arab affairs. Thus the King-Crane Commission of 1919 reported that the people of Syria and Palestine preferred the United States as their mandatory power rather than France or Great Britain. This was both a tribute to the reputation of the United States and an illustration of the truism that the "devil you don't know is better than the devil you do know."

Its image was indeed an asset as the United States entered upon its postwar role in the area. Yet it was insufficient as a basis for an active foreign policy of involvement in Arab affairs. In foreign policy, as in all other operations, the means circumscribe the ends, and new ends are only possible as new means to attain them can be created. In the Arab world the United States has been as much saddled with problems of finding instruments for its active role as with problems of defining the objectives of that role. Too often, this has been overlooked in the popular view, which tends to believe American capabilities are so massive and extensive that merely to define a national objective is to guarantee its accomplishment.

Military Power—Its Capabilities and Limitations

What then are the implements the United States has developed in dealing with Arab countries, and what are their effects on the capabilities of American diplomacy? The most direct and massive instrument the United States possesses is its military capacity. Both in its own right as the world's greatest military power and as a leader of the many nations associated with it for world security, the United States can command the support of strong allies when the question at stake is vital to all.

Military capacity was the first instrument of influence created by the United States after the war. By underwriting the military establishments of Greece and Turkey, assisting in the formation and support of CENTO, establishing bases on Middle East soil, and posting the powerful Sixth Fleet to the Mediterranean, the United States became the major armed presence in the area. This presence was created as a means not of controlling the Middle East itself, but of containing Soviet expansion. It was the protection of the Middle East, not its control, that was the chief American objective.

By the end of the second postwar decade the American military position had altered considerably. The only base left on Arab soil was in Libya, and the outlook for it had become doubtful.

The NATO and CENTO alliances in the Middle East were showing the strains of local disputes: Turkey and Greece at odds over Cyprus, Pakistan preoccupied with India, Iran professing to be threatened by the revolutionary forces of the Arab world. Missile bases in Turkey no longer had their original priority in the strategy of containing Soviet expansion. The British had left Suez, were preparing to relinquish Aden with its naval base, and it was possible that they would withdraw from the Persian Gulf in the next decade. Only the Sixth Fleet remained in its pristine strength as a massive and flexible military force, making a visible presence in Middle East affairs.

This reduced scale does not mean that the defense of the Middle East necessarily has suffered. Military weaponry and strategy have so changed that area bases have only a secondary importance as training centers and symbols of the Western commitment and presence. The armies of Iran and Turkey have not developed the expected capacity for defending the area, nor have their governments grown to a wholly reassuring state of dependable political stability. Yet these developments have been offset by the extension, range, and greater flexibility of military power. Despite a decade of growing influence, the Soviet Union has not secured military bases of its own in the area, nor does it have defense pacts with Middle East states. From a military standpoint, the defensive capacity in which United States power continues to be central is still unshaken.

How far has this military strength given the United States an effective diplomatic implement in its dealings with Arab states? The Arab world itself has no part in the American military position. With the exception of Libya, it does not house American garrisons or bases nor does it have a significant number of American military advisers or trainers. A few states (principally Jordan and Saudi Arabia) have acquired American weapons, but the United States has thus far refrained from being a major arms supplier to the Arab world. After nonalignment became the accepted foreign policy of the independent Arab states, the question of their military alliance with the West did not arise. Only the Sixth Fleet by its occasional calls to an Arab port displays the American military presence, which is thus chiefly beyond Arab borders. Whatever diplomatic leverage derives from pacts, mutual military planning, and support of military establishments is therefore minimal in the Arab world, in contrast to Turkey and Iran.

Yet although the American military position lies beyond the borders of the Arab world, it is a factor in Arab-American relations. It is the presupposition on which some of the Arab states do business with the Communist world, in the belief that should dealings with the Soviets ever threaten their independence, the United States has both the capability and the interest to prevent a takeover. If the U.A.R. should find it necessary to repudiate its massive indebtedness to the Soviets for the Aswan High Dam, and the U.S.S.R. should then move to protect its interests as Great Britain did in 1879 when it deposed the Khedive, the West under American leadership could be counted upon, the Egyptians believe, to preserve the country's independence. This contingency is distant so long as the nuclear stalemate exists; nevertheless it is not entirely absent from Arab minds. Their reliance on American power can be illustrated from conversations held by the author with a number of senior Arab officials, who made it a point to present and defend their countries' policy of opposing United States action in Viet Nam. Yet after this formal salute to their official position and its commitment to nonalignment, they said privately: "Don't get out of Viet Nam, despite our position. We count on you to contain the expansionist threat of Red China."

From the American standpoint, this response may not be a desirable diplomatic effect of its military position—but it is an unavoidable one. Far from restricting Arab actions, the American military capacity and commitment, with its balancing Soviet response, provide an element of freedom for Arab governments. Yet at the same time there is a restriction placed upon these governments. If the nuclear balance inhibits the use of Western force, it also inhibits the use of Soviet force. In this stalemate, the United States is in the better position as regards the Middle East. Its relation to the military establishments of Turkey and

Iran, the placement of its power in adjacent areas, and the presence of the Sixth Fleet mean that it could marshal force rapidly to face a major challenge or undertake a limited operation. The Soviets do not have the same flexible capacity. Only in situations where the stake justified a risk of major confrontation and possibly global conflict would they resort to military action. This was clearly shown during the 1967 Arab-Israel war, when Soviet actions were vigorous in propaganda and verbal support for the Arab cause in the Security Council and the General Assembly, but stopped short of effective military help.

Military capacity and position are clearly and basically related to the diplomatic stance of great powers interested in the Arab world. For all its apparent strength, the Soviet position is inhibited by its lack of underpinning of a flexible and present military capacity to which it can appeal in the last resort. This raises the question of whether the United States should use its power more frequently in dealing with the Arab states. Some observers have called for such specific measures as defense commitments to and joint military planning with Israel, and for more active support of Saudi Arabia in its conflict with the U.A.R. over Yemen. Others have suggested that there should be recurring displays of force (on the pattern of the landing in Lebanon) as a reminder to the Arabs that the United States can and will act directly when it chooses to do so. In essence, such views would have the United States assume the traditional British role of policing the area, with side-arms always on display.

The role sounds attractive as an easy solution to American problems with the Arabs, and one which some believe to be in keeping with the attributes of a great power. But it is unrealistic from the standpoint both of the United States and of the Arab world. The United States has so multiplied its global commitments in recent years that it cannot use a military response lightly or repeatedly. While the probability of direct military confrontation with the Soviets has lessened in general, the United States does not want to push the U.S.S.R. into situations in the Middle East where it may feel forced to take a harder and more active role.

Nor is there any reason to suppose that diplomacy based directly upon military force will be effective in Arab-American dealings. However much the Arab states are in conflict among themselves, they would close ranks in the face of a direct threat from a great power, which they would interpret as an attempt to revive colonial controls, as witness the general Arab reaction to the 1956 Anglo-French invasion. When the U.A.R. closed the Gulf of Aqaba in 1967, some advocated immediate and (if necessary) unilateral American action to break the blockade, even if this meant shooting a passage through the Straits of Tiran. But an American military clash with Egypt, especially on behalf of Israel, would have caused an immediate, unified, and bitter response from all Arab states, leaving the United States in an even worse position with the Arabs than it occupied after the Arab-Israel war, bad as that was. Moreover, the Arab world has its own place in international affairs, with direct participation in the United Nations and useful connection with the Afro-Asian group, to which the thirteen votes of the Arab world are important. This group would have strongly supported the Arabs and taken measures against American interests had American force been used.

Clearly, in the Arab world (as elsewhere) the very size and responsibilities of American military power limits its use in daily diplomacy. Arab leaders are realistically aware of this, and repeated threats or gestures of force are not apt to bend them to the American will. The power and position of the United States continues to provide a major element in the defense of the Middle East from external threat. It has forced the Soviets to pursue a policy in the Arab world not based upon threats of force. It is the general backdrop against which American policy can be formulated—but it is not an instrument directly applicable to daily diplomacy and it will not protect American interests from many of the vexing problems which beset them.

Leadership and the United Nations

Military capacity is only one aspect of the influential role of the United States in international affairs. In the past, American leadership in the Western alliance has given it influence in the policies of its allies relating to Arab affairs. American representations were partly responsible for the British agreement in 1955 to withdraw their troops from Egypt. U.S. refusal to take part in financing the Aswan High Dam in 1956 was followed by the withdrawal of the British and World Bank offers. To take a contrasting example, the American decision to support a stabilization loan to the U.A.R. in 1962 elicited additional support from Great Britain, Germany, and Italy. Because of its commanding position in the International Monetary Fund, the United States at times could press for conditions on the Fund's operations which reflected American economic foreign policy. In the United Nations, the United States is not only a permanent member of the Security Council, but has been the center of a wide group of allied and friendly states.

At times this position of leadership has been a significant diplomatic instrument, but it is one whose effectiveness has been decreasing. Support from America's traditional allies is not so unwavering as formerly, as is shown by the steadily shrinking inclination to follow the United States' lead in keeping Communist China out of the world organization. Within the Western alliance there has been a loosening of political bonds, evident in the Middle East as well as in Europe or in Viet Nam: witness the refusal of the British government despite strenuous American efforts to recognize the republican regime of Yemen, and the independent approach of France to Arab-Israel problems.

Nor has the United States found in the United Nations the most effective means for dealing with the Arab world. Many of its problems with Arab states are too specific and limited to generate United Nations action. Others, if submitted, would run into general Afro-Asian opposition. Arab governments not only have their own position, but can appeal for support to the swelling number of new states in the General Assembly. Economic and technical assistance is too central to American diplomacy to be surrendered entirely to international auspices—and there is no evidence that the United Nations (under its existing machinery) could more effectively administer aid. Only in peace-keeping operations has the United States consistently used the instrumentality of the world organization. It has been a constant supporter of (and financial contributor to) U.N. operations attempting to contain and end the Arab-Israel conflicts, although this has not prevented the United States from taking unilateral action in the form of arms sales to the contending parties in the argument. In the Yemen dispute the United States was the principal mover for mounting a U.N. observer force, in the hope that this would hasten disengagement. In Cyprus it has strongly and consistently supported U.N. action. With the outbreak of Arab-Israel hostilities in 1967, the United States sought in the Security Council its chief instrument for securing a cease-fire.

In short, the United States has sought from the United Nations an interposing presence in Middle East disputes, thus freeing itself from the necessity of undertaking that role. As disputes continue (and possibly multiply) this aspect of American diplomatic policy can be expected to increase. In the ominous disarray prefacing the launching of the new South Arabian state into independence, the United States both voiced its direct concern and supported efforts in the United Nations to bring the situation before that body. Peace-keeping operations of the United Nations have been heavily financed by the United States, but the cost of using this instrument is less than direct American action would be and the international character of the operations protects the United States from appearing as a "neocolonial" power in the area.

Mutual Interests and Persuasion

In a broad sense, diplomacy is conducted by two sets of instruments—those of pressure and those of persuasion. Military capacity, a leading position in international affairs, and use of the policing machinery of the United Nations are chiefly instruments of pressure. Their use is limited to major crises, and they are not apt to be the principal elements of American foreign policy in its daily dealings with Arab countries. In consequence, the United States has relied mostly on persuasion in its relations with Arab governments. To be sure, the line between pressure and persuasion is indistinct. Persuasion may contain an element of pressure—at least the capacity to apply pressure may make the persuasion more persuasive. Yet the two are different in concept. Pressure rests upon the ability of one government to force its demands upon another by some form of coercion. Persuasion is built upon a mutuality of interests between governments, where action is undertaken because both parties benefit from it. When the mutuality of interests is in a vital area of national interest and leads to deep and continuing involvement, it may create a pressure of its own—but it is different from pressure involved in military or dominant political power.

Thus a basic American problem has been to discover and cultivate those mutual interests which may exist between it and the Arab world. This is not an easy or simple exercise. There is a basic difference between the frames of reference within which the United States and many Arab countries place their problems. It has already been noted that the United States became active in the Middle East because of a situation outside the area— the global problem of world security and the containment of Soviet-Communist expansion. Inevitably the United States has viewed many Arab developments primarily in relation to the beyond-the-area-interest, and only secondarily as focused upon internal conditions within Arab states themselves. A revolution in Iraq, Soviet support for the U.A.R. in Yemen, Arab activities in the Afro-Asian group, visits of Kuwait officials to Communist China, have been measured against their possible effect on the world balance more than against their effect on the life of the Arab world itself.

In contrast, the Arab states are preoccupied with their own immediate problems. In addition to their economic concerns, they are countries entering upon a new stage of economic and social development. Like the United States in its infant days, their most pressing problem is the new frontier—not an unexplored region of virgin plains and forests, but new possibilities of utilizing human and material resources for modernization and progress. American policy is partly judged in the light of how it is related to this problem. To the U.A.R., the struggle in Yemen was viewed in terms of its effect on the modernizing of the Arab world, the success of the revolutionary regime and system, and the credibility of a U.A.R. commitment to a sister revolutionary state. That the struggle might ultimately strengthen the Soviet position in the area, expand the Chinese Communist presence, and lead to instability in neighboring states, was not of vital concern to them. Yet the United States cannot overlook such possibilities because they are related to its larger and global objectives.

In other words, there is often a clash of priorities between the United States and Arab governments. Where the former places containment and diminution of Soviet-Communist expansion and influence first, the latter place containment and diminution of Israel. The United States gives high priority to tranquility and stability in the Middle East; the Arab revolutionary movement is more interested in the rebirth of the Arab world into a new pattern, even though this may involve conflict with conservative neighbors. The United States would like to see orderly and evolutionary progress toward modernization; many groups within the Arab world, as well as the radical governments, believe that a revolutionary upheaval is the inescapable prelude to the new future. Whatever mutuality of interests may be found between the United States and the Arabs, it exists within a framework of basic differences. Both parties realistically must accept this fact if a mutually useful relationship is to be sustained. The United States cannot base its policy on the assumption that Arab states will agree with it on basic concerns, so many of which lie outside their borders. Nor can Arab governments expect the United States to formulate policy only in relation to what the Arabs believe to be good for themselves. Somewhere between the two extremes lies the area in which a mutuality of interests must be sought.

The range and character of mutual interests vary from country to country. Lebanon, Saudi Arabia, and Jordan, with their free enterprise systems, economic involvement with the West, and pro-Western nonalignment offer a different setting for persuasive diplomacy than do Iraq, Syria, and the U.A.R. Nevertheless, the latter have interests of their own in which the United States shares. Their retention of independence and freedom of action despite close association with the Soviets, the development of political stability amidst revolutionary change, and the success of their attack on social and economic problems are concerns in which the United States has a stake. Thus there are multiple and sometimes conflicting sets of mutual interests within the Arab world which produce multiple American diplomatic approaches. Thoroughly to appraise these and the instruments of persuasion available for them would require a detailed study of each Arab country.

The Uses of Aid

There are certain general implements which serve a mutuality of interests and have been available to the United States in its dealings with the Arab countries. The first of these is aid—military, economic, and technical—which has become a dimension of postwar foreign policy. Not only is it used by Western countries in the Arab world, and by the Soviets and their allies, but some Arab governments themselves are turning to it. The U.A.R. has supplied arms to Cyprus, military trainers to Algeria, technicians to many Arab and a few African countries, and has provided some credits to stimulate trade and economic development in states where it has an interest. The Kuwait Development Fund is financing some significant improvement programs in sister Arab countries.

The United States has used limited amounts of military aid in the area. It has made selected weapons available to Israel, Jordan, Saudi Arabia, and a few other countries (in much smaller quantities). Its financial support, moreover, has made possible the maintenance of the Jordanian army, whose cost could not be borne by that country alone without catastrophic effects on its economy. Military aid is the reflection partly of strategic interests (Jordan as a counterbalance to Israel, Saudi Arabia in relation to petroleum), partly of a concern to discourage intra-area conflict (making Israel secure against Arab attacks, Saudi

Arabia against U.A.R. pressure), partly of support for pro-Western nonalignment. It is evidence of a mutuality of interests already in existence which it serves to encourage and support. Yet nowhere in the Arab world does the United States have the direct and major relation to military establishments that it has had in Turkey, Greece, and Iran. Although diplomatically useful, military aid is only a limited and localized instrument of American diplomacy toward Arab countries.

American economic aid and technical assistance in the Arab world embrace a variety of programs. In recent years one of the most important has been the sale of surplus commodities under Public Law 480, a principal element in United States relations with the U.A.R., the republican regime of Yemen, and Algeria. From the proceeds of these sales, local-currency loans at modest interest rates are made to the development programs of the host country. Dollar loans are also made, either directly by the American aid agency, or through such international organizations as the World Bank and the International Monetary Fund. Occasionally the United States has made direct grants—Jordan has been a major recipient—to support an urgently needed development project. Technicians and consultants for launching new programs or assisting at a critical stage in programs already under way have also been supplied. Technical information, such as that concerning the desalinization of sea water, is made available in countries which need it. Although these activities have not spread uniformly across the Arab world, the principal Arab states have all benefited, in some form and at some time.

The justification for such economic assistance is that it serves the mutual interests of the United States and the recipient country. What these interests are, and the problems they create, will be considered later; here the character of economic and technical aid as an instrument of diplomacy is appraised.

There is much popular (and congressional) unrealism as to what may be expected from foreign aid. Many would mark its effectiveness by the sense of gratitude it generates and the "friendly support" of American policies it produces. Others believe that it can be an instrument of overt pressure. One American senator, for instance, proposed that the price of PL 480 wheat to the U.A.R. should be that country's recognition of the state of Israel, his argument being that American food was so indispensable to Egyptians that they would pay the price of national honor, as they see it, to secure it.

Such expectations are based upon a failure to recognize the facts of life about economic aid. For one thing, in the Arab world no American aid program has been large enough to dominate the local economy. Jordan may be the exception; the combination of economic aid with military and political support is the major element in the country's continued existence. The oil-producing states of Saudi Arabia, Kuwait, and Iraq have ample financial resources of their own. Their problem is technical development rather than financial assistance. The countries which need economic help most—the U.A.R., Syria, Yemen—are the most difficult to provide with broad economic support, largely because their attitudes and activities pose so many difficulties for the United States. Moreover, where Soviet competition is active, neither the West nor the East has been able to build an exclusive position as the supplier of aid. If both were to stop their programs simultaneously, the result would be disastrous, but the supposition is highly unlikely. The U.A.R. has been the largest recipient of the largest quantity of American aid in the Arab world (chiefly in the form of food purchased by local currency). Yet for all its size and importance, American aid at its height contributed less than one-tenth to the total national economy. The ending of U.S. aid caused Egypt to be faced with a most serious problem, but it did not result in the immediate collapse of the economy, partly because some limited Soviet aid was made available, partly because the country tightened its belt and revised some of its economic goals.

The expectation that economic aid is so important that it constitutes an instrument of diplomatic pressure is not realistic. The record of Soviet aid makes this clear. That aid has been massive in some countries and often is connected with projects of marked visibility (such as the Aswan High Dam) or with national security. Yet the Soviets, through their aid programs, have had little more success than the Americans in securing direct support of some of their most important interests or in dominating the policies of their clients. A collection of comments from Soviet economists and planners (1964–65) contained complaints about the lack of political results of Russian aid which could pass as excerpts from the speeches of American congressmen. Despite its size and importance in the U.A.R. and Syria, Soviet military and economic aid was not able to buy permission for and recognition of a Communist party in these countries. When Premier Khrushchev visited the U.A.R. in May of 1964 to join in inaugurating the first stage of the High Dam, Soviet Embassy officials complained that the local press was not being properly grateful to the U.S.S.R. for its generous aid. "You would think to read the papers," said one of them, "that this is an Egyptian, not a Russian dam. How do you Americans get the U.A.R. to be grateful for your help?"

The fact is that aid does not automatically generate gratitude which can be translated into political action. There may be a measure of gratitude where an aid program is sufficiently public and connected with a widespread need. Both Soviet aid for the High Dam and American supply of wheat and corn have been recognized by Egyptians as a contribution to their welfare. But whatever sense of gratitude such projects produce is a negligible political force. The recipients judge that the donors of aid are not moved mainly by disembodied philanthropy, but are seeking their own interests. The massive resources of aid-supplying countries compared to those of the recipients are such that no sacrifice on the donor's part is acknowledged.

Underlying the attitude of countries emerging from a colonial past is the widespread feeling that the international community has a responsibility to assist them. The first demand of dependent peoples is for political freedom—a right they regard as owed to them by the world community. Now there is a new demand: the right to technical development and the assistance necessary to achieve it. Medicine, science, industry, economic growth are no longer viewed as ex-gratia gifts of the wealthier nations, but as obligations owed by the world to its emerging peoples. In some sense this help is regarded as compensation for past exploitation in which the resources of colonial areas were developed or controlled by foreign powers without adequate payment. Consequently the gratitude which may be created by even a large aid program is muted, and cannot be expected to produce direct support for the interests of the donor country.

If gratitude does not produce support for the donor's interests, it has been argued that continuing need can bring that result. When the assistance is sufficiently valuable, its contribution to the local economy will force the recipient government to give attention to sustaining those relations with the donor which make aid possible. This is not the same as attaching direct political conditions to aid, for the pressure arises out of the nature of the aid relationship, as the receiving country discovers that its actions and policies affect the ability of the contributing government to continue assistance. Aid is thus seen as a form of pressure generated by enlightened self-interest which will dampen disputes between the countries involved and prod the host government to be forthcoming in those aspects of its conduct which might adversely affect the aid program.

In fact this has seldom happened, or has happened to a lesser degree than the United States hoped. Several factors are involved: for instance, the nature of the assistance given and the length of commitment it entails. Food sales, which may be important economically to the recipient country, are quickly consumed and do not involve several years of relationship to produce dividends. In contrast, a project like the High Dam requires a decade for its completion, and an interruption of aid during the building period would leave the host country with a visible and unfinished task which it could not complete by itself. Consequently, PL 480 food assistance, though needed and wanted by the Egyptians, has not had the same potential for sustaining good relations as projects like the High Dam.

Another factor is how vital a specific aid project is to a country's development. Aside from the supply of food, few American projects have been so basic to a nation's economy that the government would alter its policies to continue them. Too often aid-giving nations have argued that economic necessity will paper over political difficulties—as the Anglo-Iranian Oil Company's belief that the royalties paid to the Iranian government were so essential to the country that it would not take a politically motivated step of nationalizing oil, thereby cutting off its economic nose to spite its political face. That belief was proved false, as has been the hope that for the sake of receiving aid a country will always refrain from actions of which its donor disapproves.

Yet such actions and policies have often resulted in the diminution or cessation of aid. On the donor's side, there is an expectation of immediate results and a failure to recognize the aggressive sensitivity of recipient governments to any hint of pressure. When a quick political response to an aid program is not forthcoming, Washington officials may grow weary in their efforts or find that they cannot secure the necessary congressional appropriations. Many Arab leaders do not fully understand the nature of the political process in the United States or the problems of the President and Secretary of State in securing support for a program which is paid for by congressional action.

An illustration in an extreme form is the American aid relationship with the U.A.R. From 1960 through 1965, the United States was forthcoming in its aid program, of which the largest element was the sale for local currency of food badly needed by Egypt. It was hoped that a mutuality of interests would be created which would maintain good relations between the two countries. Yet by 1967, the aid program had virtually ceased, largely because the U.A.R. did not make possible its continuance. The U.A.R. leadership has seemed unable to grasp the fact that American aid to a country with which it had had serious differences can not be sustained unless the recipient country takes some pain to cultivate good relations on its own responsibility.

At times the factor which interrupted the relationship was not a major policy difference. Realistic diplomacy recognizes that nations differ in matters where they consider their national security seriously involved, and that no aid program is likely to change such policy. Often the difficulty comes from lesser matters —a public speech by the head of state, lethargy in responding to requests or paying agreed compensation, or government-inspired newspaper campaigns without particular political pertinency. The image of hostility and irresponsibility such actions create makes it difficult to secure favorable congressional support for aid appropriations—and the interests of both the giving and the receiving countries suffer. It is especially difficult to elicit a reasonable relationship when aid is in the form of food. Food is so vital, so personal, so connected with basic human needs, that conditions, restrictions and fluctuations in supplying it arouse violent reactions. Any suspicion that food is being used for political ends robs the assistance of much of its diplomatic usefulness, as has been shown in the reactions of the U.A.R. and India to the delay and curtailment of American food sales.

Yet economic assistance does offer opportunities for persuasive diplomacy. It is unrealistic to assume that dramatic policy shifts can be expected as the result of a specific aid program. The moment it appears that a government must be made to pay in public political action for the aid received, the price becomes too high for national pride and the utility of the operation suffers. If that pitfall is avoided, there can be a continuing process of adjustment with small but cumulative gains. Persuasive diplomacy utilizing the aid relationship on more than one occasion has led to moderation of policies and actions in the Arab world. Whether the gains finally justify the aid expenditure is to be determined only in the light of the donor country's interest and objectives. Where gains are made, they cannot be put on public display without imperiling the continuation of the process of adjustment.

The problem will increase as the American aid program becomes more restrictive and selective. Not only may there be mounting pressure for a closer connection of aid with political objectives, but the attitude of the recipient country toward the United States will play a larger and more determinative role. Congress is apt to have a short temper with those aid-receiving governments which unnecessarily create difficulties in their daily dealings with America. The imminent reduction of American food surpluses will affect what has been the most flexible kind of aid and the easiest to provide. When surplus wheat is bursting from American elevators, it is hard to argue against its use abroad in the national interest, even in countries which occasion the United States continuing difficulty. But when this surplus is exhausted and the United States has to expand cultivation to grow wheat specifically for export, generally against payment in local currency, a country like the U.A.R. can expect that a reasonable and cooperative relation with the United States will take high priority in the persuasion.

A further diplomatic effect of the aid relationship is the dialogue it creates, despite political differences. The more tension there is between American and Arab interests, the more difficult it is to sustain a meaningful contact. At times American diplomatic missions in some Arab countries have been islands, isolated from the mainland of mutual interest, and only to be brought in contact with it by the most strenuous efforts. Every diplomatic conversation is apt to begin, continue and end with points of difference, of which American support for Israel is an unvarying ingredient. Yet the essence of diplomatic representation is dialogue—the continuous exchange of views through which the attitudes of two governments are clarified and points of mutual concern developed. The least a diplomat can do is to talk to the government to which he is accredited—and there have been times in Arab-American relations when talk with the higher circles of government has been exceedingly sparse.

Here the economic relationship is invaluable. It deals with matters important to the recipient nation's welfare, and should not be directly enmeshed in political questions. More nearly than any other device, it helps make possible what has been called the "ice box" approach to binational relations—an approach based on a mutual recognition that there are divergencies of policies between two countries which will not be changed easily or rapidly. Instead of making these a subject of constant and fruitless recrimination, the difference can be frankly recognized, the topic "put in the ice box" (at least when it is not in a critical phase), and attention turned to other interests where there is a mutuality of benefit. These other interests are economic and developmental in many Arab countries. An effective aid program involving continued negotiation of projects carries the diplomat into the daily workings of the host government and gives its officials a point of justified contact with him. Where an aid program is important, its director, next to the ambassador, has the widest entrée to the country and enjoys a continuous contact with its government, which is difficult for a political officer to obtain.

Cultural Interchange

Another implement available to American diplomacy is found in the general interest of the Arab world in Western culture and the large American resources in this field. As in many other parts of the world, Arab youth responds to the Western cinema, current music, clothing styles, imported TV programs, and modern folkways. But there is a more basic and important interest in Western culture as a state of mind—the broad aspects of intellectual life, the processes it uses, the values it pursues, the modes by which it is expressed, the institutions in which it flourishes.

Here two aspects must be noted about the cultural situation in the Arab world. The first is that despite postwar political changes, the momentum of intellectual development still carries the Arab world toward the West. This is due in part to the fact that historically Islamic and Western culture are of a piece. Islam, the religious framework in which Arab culture developed, is sister to Judaism and Christianity, and its most basic concepts are rooted in the same Semitic sources. Medieval European Christian and Arab Muslim scholars drew many of their intellectual materials from the same corpus of classical writing—Plato, Aristotle, Plotinus—and Arab and Muslim intellectual life has never been "oriental" or "eastern" in the sense that Indian, Chinese, and Japanese thought has been.

To this commonality of historic development is added the impact of the modern Western world in the Arab cultural awakening of the past century. It was to politically dominant Western Europe that the Arab turned for his new patterns of literature, science, education, and institutions. The modern intellectual leaders were trained in Western universities, and on the pattern of that training the modern Arab educational institutions were established. French and English have become the second languages of the Arab intellectual elite. As a result, the modern Arab mind is basically Western in its approach to many problems, and in the materials and concepts it uses—even when Western political institutions have been repudiated. Leaders like Nasser, King Hussein, Bourguiba, and the technicians who operate their societies are essentially Western in the framework of their thinking. The Arab university community remains rooted in the Western tradition and is struggling to keep open its intellectual entrée to the West against the pressures sometimes generated by politically anti-Western Arab governments.

The second significant fact about Arab culture is that its patterns and outlook are more fluid today than they have been for many centuries. Decades of penetration by modern technology, education, economic organization, and cultural life have indeed created a Western outlook, at the same time they have deeply eroded the traditional forms of historic Muslim culture. With the rise of nationalism and its embodiment in political independence, the question is now sharply raised as to the relation between the inherited culture and modern innovation. National pride emphasizes the heritage of the past—as in the demand of Arab educators for a distinctly "Arab" form and content for the new national universities. Yet the desire for modernization, progress, and recognition sets a premium on those very cultural developments which most challenge and alter the Arab past. Thus a leading modern Arab thinker wrote to his compatriots: "We must erase from our minds the evil suggestion that there is an Eastern and Western mentality."

With the needs created by independence, the conflict between modernity and the past has been raised more to the level of the conscious. New governments must provide systems of national education, technical training, and popular culture. In the more radical states the repudiation of the economic and political systems of the past means that there is a conscious search for new patterns of national life which will provide rapid progress. In all states the demand for modernization and economic development overrides the loyalty to past ways. Despite much that is being said in Arab circles about the adaptability of historic institutions to modern needs, in fact the demands of the developing society lead to pragmatic choices in which the Islamic inheritance plays only a minor role.

This choice is being exercised in a world which offers new technical and cultural possibilities. With the rise and progress of the Communist system, the West no longer is regarded as the sole custodian of progress. Communist cultural and technical developments not only offer an alternative to traditional Western ways, but have the advantage of a certain freshness and novelty which may attract countries seeking new devices of rapid development. The attraction is sometimes aided by the commitment to nonalignment which provides a *raison d'être* for using the cultural patterns from both West and East. Nonaligned developing countries seek technical assistance wherever it can be found— and in the wake of such assistance there is an extended intellectual and cultural interaction. The point is illustrated by the complaint of a group of young Egyptian univeristy graduates who were assigned to work with Soviet technicians on the High Dam. Before their assignment they were planning to take graduate engineering studies in the United States. Now, they said, "not only is our chance to study in America indefinitely postponed, but if it ever comes, it will be hard for us to profit by it. Six or seven years of work with the Russians will cast our engineering skills in the Soviet pattern—and it will be too late to change to another system." Their concern was not political indoctrination, but technical orientation. Foreign technicians, equipment, and projects carry with them an unavoidable intellectual impact which becomes an element in the emerging culture of the future Arab world.

The question at stake is what kind of intellectual concepts and values will govern the coming Arab generation. Twenty years hence the young university students and technicians of today will be the leaders and key men of Arab society. Will they act within a general acceptance of Western thought and values? Despite the political differences of the present and the general repudiation of Western political control, those who now head Arab society are still to some degree Western men, and a continuing and comprehensible dialogue can be maintained with them, to the advantage of both parties. If this connection is lost to a future generation, the estrangement between the Arab world and the West will be deepened, with less of a common meeting ground.

Thus the United States must not overlook nor underestimate the potential of its cultural cooperation with the Arab world. Specific patterns of development will differ from country to country, but in every society there is a lively interest in Western life and important groups supporting it. To make available to them the best and most useful resources of American technical, intellectual, educational, and cultural experience is to serve the needs of both the Arabs and the United States. Yet in doing this the American must recognize that cultural cooperation stands in a category of influence different from that of military strength or economic aid. It cannot be used for political pressure, making conformity to a desired policy the price of scholarships, exchanges, or technicians. It cannot be imposed but must grow from and utilize the felt needs and aspirations of the other society. Its object is not to reproduce the American system of education, economic organization, or culture, but to make available to societies reshaping their own culture in the pattern they themselves choose, those elements of Western experience which best serve their objectives. Its effects are quiet and long-term, and its programs transcend the fluctuations of political relations. Many of its operations must be carried on by private agencies with the freedom from government control that is the hallmark of American intellectual life.

For this task the United States has impressive resources. A century of philanthropic service in the Middle East created American schools, colleges, hospitals, and rural programs identified in the Arab mind as pioneers of progress. Robert College in Istanbul, the American University at Beirut, and the American University at Cairo have been respected and influential educational centers, where the best of American and Middle East scholarship meet on the common ground of intellectual cooperation for national service. The multiplicity and diversity of universities in the United States offer training in every conceivable field of technical and intellectual development. Exchange programs bring American teachers to Arab institutions, and Arab scholars and students to the United States. The unique programs of industrial training by American manufacturers offer a dimension of education practically unknown and badly needed in the Arab world. Private foundations and voluntary agencies, such as the Ford Foundation, the Rockefeller Foundation, the Near East Foundation, and the International Voluntary Service, carry on programs which are eagerly welcomed. The Department of State has its Bureau of Educational and Cultural Affairs, and every embassy has a cultural officer.

Despite such potential, American cultural opportunity in the Arab world has been utilized only partially. One reason is that the United States Information Agency, in charge of activities in the field, is often caught between its function as a propaganda agency and its cultural responsibilities. It seems difficult for Congress to realize the importance of the latter. One senator visiting Cairo dismissed the cultural program of the Embassy by asking: "Why is it necessary to prove to Egyptians that we too can dance on our toes?" Such an uncomprehending and uninformed view of the value and substance of cultural cooperation is reflected in the limited budgets given USIA and the Department of State for their cultural activities and in the restrictions placed on the use of counterpart funds. Another difficulty lies in the lack of effective partnership between private agencies and the government. Specific projects in the field are supported by government-financed contracts with universities, but too often that support is short-term and hedged in by innumerable restrictions. Moreover, these contracts do little to utilize the capacities of universities within this country to train foreign students. Beset with increasing pressure from the swelling American academic population, universities lack the resources to offer foreign students the assistance which many of them need. In the field of industrial training little has been done. The United States could well follow the lead of Germany, which annually brings in several hundred young Arabs for technical training in German factories.

*   *   *

It is clear from this brief audit of the instruments of American diplomacy that the chief influence of the United States in the Arab world must be wielded by persuasion and devotion to mutual interests. Overt pressure or repeated threats of force will not induce the Arabs to form a Friends of America Club. If the most vital American security interests are threatened, the military capacity of the United States is adequate to protect them. But for sustained and helpful relations there must be a growing sense of mutual needs and of the value to both parties in cooperating to meet them. On no other basis will Americans and Arabs understand and work with each other.

Yet it is just here that the problem arises. One should not be misled into thinking that because such instruments of persuasive diplomacy exist, they can be used to obliterate the strain in American-Arab relations resulting from deep-seated and fundamental differences in national policies and interests. Of these differences, the most ubiquitous, emotional and basic lies in the Arab-Israel conflict. So long as the United States appears to Arab eyes in the image of the creator and sustainer of Israel, gains made through economic and cultural cooperation will be fleeting. (The avalanche of anti-American feeling which swept the Arab world as a result of the 1967 Arab-Israel war demonstrated their evanescence.) This does not mean that the implements of persuasive diplomacy should be discarded, but it does mean that they are not a substitute for the resolution of basic issues between Arab states and the United States, of which the Arab-Israel dispute is at the forefront.

Chapter V

Guidelines for Policy

American policy toward the Middle East has been criticized as being at best inconsistent, at worst nonexistent. Both accusations arise from the apparent lack of a single policy toward the area as a whole. The United States has strongly supported pro-Western commitment in the northern tier (Turkey, Iran, Pakistan) but has been content to accept and sometimes to aid nonalignment in the Arab world. It has used its influence to keep the Soviet presence out of some Middle Eastern states, while backing others which welcome Communist assistance. It has simultaneously supported conservative, free-enterprise governments and revolutionary, socialist regimes. At some periods it has sought to use a "chosen instrument" to serve its interests in the Arab world; at other times it has maintained neutrality toward all Arab leaders. Even within the limits of relations with individual countries its approach has frequently shifted. There have been four major policies toward Egypt in the last fifteen years, and the end does not yet seem to be in sight. It is little wonder that some Arab leaders say they prefer to deal with Great Britain rather than the United States because "bad as they are, we always know what position the British will take, but we are never quite sure of the Americans."

This record is sometimes cited as one more illustration of vacillating pragmatism in the State Department, which is accused of being more concerned with immediate solutions to daily problems than with sustaining a consistent and long-range policy. Yet the fact is that even with more imagination and effort it is almost impossible to formulate a single policy toward the "Middle East" or the "Arab world." As has already been noted, the two concepts are nebulous and elusive, offering no clearly defined target for policy formulation. The eighteen major states which compose the Middle East have different foreign policies and are differently related to American interests, both general and specific; and the states are themselves rapidly changing and are often inconsistent in their own actions. Moreover, the interests of the United States in the Middle East have expanded and altered, being constantly affected by external issues of global policy and security. Under such conditions it is premature and probably dangerous to seek a single and consistent policy embracing the entire Middle East.

Yet it is wrong to conclude that the American approach to Middle Eastern problems has been, or must be, formless and without direction. If there can be no single policy for the area as a whole, there is a frame of reference within which tactical policy decisions toward individual countries have been made, drawing upon general conditions in the area, the vital interests of the United States, and the diplomatic implements available to it. These are cardinal points in relation to which courses of action are plotted, rather than detailed sailing charts. In policy decisions toward specific countries with specific problems, they are basic considerations against which other elements of the situation must be weighed. Such points of reference may loosely be called "tactical guidelines," and policy should not overstep them except by deliberate choice and after careful judgment. Rarely announced in policy statements, they may best be identified by a comprehensive review of the ensemble of individual policies during a given period.

As conditions in the Middle East and the relationship of the United States to them have changed, the guidelines have changed. Prior to the Suez crisis, the United States was frequently a junior partner to Great Britain, and the Soviet penetration of the area had just begun. American policy then appeared to be guided by the necessity of building strength in the area, and thus of supporting the British position, favoring some Middle East countries without alienating others, and maintaining cordial relations with all. It is clear in retrospect that these guidelines led to serious dilemmas which the United States resolved only partially and temporarily.

After the Suez crisis of 1956, the United States had to review its approach to Arab affairs. Great Britain no longer played a leading role in the area, Soviet penetration became wider and appeared more permanent, and the instruments available to American diplomacy required reappraisal. The Kennedy administration sought to introduce into foreign policy new tactics, if not always a new strategy, which led to a revision of policy guidelines for dealing with Arab affairs. The new position contained many elements of the old, but they were recast into more positive form and more closely related to the capabilities of American diplomacy. During the Kennedy years the guidelines were more consistently followed and more successfully upheld against domestic critics than previously. The Johnson administration continued to follow the same approach in theory, but in fact both its style of diplomacy and the altered situation in which it operated made for less consistency in applying them. No new guidelines appeared, partly because those in existence derived from facts and considerations which continued to be valid.

The Arab-Israel war of 1967 radically changed the situation. Bitter resentment against the United States dominated the Arab mind and seven countries broke off their relations with America. The flow of Arab oil to Great Britain and the United States was interrupted, some American properties were attacked, others sequestered, and a boycott of American business was threatened. The use of many of the instruments on which the United States had depended for its relations with the Arab world (chiefly economic and cultural assistance) had to be suspended—some possibly for a long period. Opinion in the United States became generally unfavorable to the Arab world, making it difficult to take new initiatives in rebuilding relations with Arab countries. Inevitably the guidelines which had been followed were subject to intensive review and revision to meet new conditions and the still unknown problems of the future. Yet the basic elements on which American tactics had been based continue to exist and in some form must be taken into account in plotting a new course of action.

Aid and Its Rationale

The first guideline is that the United States, within the limits of its financial and legislative ability, in assisting Middle East countries undertaking economic and social development, will do so without regard to the system of government or economics followed. This does not imply that assistance will be given to any country requesting or needing it; for if that were done, the entire Middle East could well be on the American payroll. Aid funds are limited, and their allocation necessarily must be affected by the particular interests of the United States in the country requesting aid, and by the effects of the aid program on the general situation in the Middle East. The significance of the guideline lies in its final clause: that aid will be given *without regard to the system of government or economics followed* by the recipient country. Conformity to a political or economic system favored by the United States is thus removed from the preconditions of receiving American assistance. The question may be raised whether an avowedly Communist government would be helped. At the moment the question is theoretical, since there are no such governments in the Middle East, and none seems likely to emerge in the near future. Yet circumstances in the Middle East are conceivable in which a country would receive assistance on the pattern of American aid to Yugoslavia. But the guideline was not framed with this possibility in view, and it must be understood against the background of the diversities of the Middle East as they exist today.

Obviously, American aid was being extended to countries having different systems before this guideline made the matter explicit. From the beginning, aid programs have responded to situations where a vital American concern was at stake, regardless of the particular nature of the government. Prior to 1960 assistance was given to Lebanon (free-enterprise republic), Iraq (feudal oligarchy), Morocco (traditional monarchy), Israel (democracy with a socialist trend), Jordan (army-based monarchy with a traditional elite), Greece (constitutional, democratic, monarchial), Tunisia (mildy socialist), Egypt (at first a traditional monarchy, then revolutionary), Syria (republic with rising army control), Libya (traditional tribal monarchy), Turkey (republic with government economic control), and Afghanistan (feudal monarchy). Many of these programs have now been terminated either because they lacked economic justification or because the attitudes and policies of the host governments made it difficult to continue them.

Why, then, the necessity for a new guideline on aid? Because the diversity of governments and economic systems in the Middle East has been accentuated sharply in recent years. The rise of revolutionary movements and their embodiment in the radical regimes of the United Arab Republic, Syria, Iraq, and Algeria have posed the question of the American attitude toward other than traditional or Western-type political and economic systems. Because these regimes have welcomed Soviet assistance and adopted aspects of socialist policies, many have concluded that they have entered the Soviet orbit and retreated from the West. They are also in dispute or tension with the traditional governments of the area, a situation which puts the United States under pressure to decide whether to support one system against the other.

Thus, the earlier concern to maintain cordial relations with all governments of the area has been sharpened and complicated. It was not difficult to supply aid to traditional Iran (a non-Arab state) and to post-monarchial Egypt during the opening years of its revolution. Both governments appeared then to be searching for an evolutionary course of progress and were not in conflict with each other. Later the United Arab Republic's Arab socialism stood at the quite opposite pole from Iran's anti-radical evolution. The two countries are not only mutually hostile (diplomatic relations were broken in 1961) but represent systems struggling to destroy each other. They also represent opposing political attitudes toward the West and the United States, Iran being pro-Western and aligned by treaty, the U.A.R. anti-Western and nonaligned. It is in the face of such situations that the new guideline of political and economic neutrality in giving aid was developed.

There are four principal reasons for the guideline. The first is the need for stability in Middle Eastern governments, a condition already reviewed in relation to American interests in the area. Violent change, no matter in which Middle Eastern state it may occur, complicates intra-area relations, invites foreign interference, and may set off a chain reaction of upheaval in neighboring countries. The interests both of the Middle East and of the United States require reasonable tranquility while the area is seeking its uneasy way into new patterns of modernization and development.

Lack of economic and social progress is a growing threat to stability. The shift in political power away from the old elite toward the emerging middle class and their leaders, the rising tide of expectation among the masses, the popular identification of "modernization" with rapid progress in solving the age-old problems of poverty, ignorance, and disease, all make it mandatory for any Middle Eastern government to achieve reasonable improvement or risk downfall. Even the remoteness of Abu Dhabi (the tiny, newly rich sheikhdom on the Persian Gulf) did not save its medieval ruler from forced abdication because of his indifference to progress. Younger members of the family took over because "we need a deep water port, an international airport, hospitals, schools and town planning, plus some parks for the people. From now on the people will reap the fruits of our prosperity."*

Insofar as an aid program assists the host government to achieve reasonable progress, it assists in maintaining stability. Whether that stability is in a conservative, Western-oriented

* *Time,* August 19, 1966.

state, or in a revolutionary state with Soviet connections, it is still stability and valuable in its own right. In some revolutionary states the probable alternative to present regimes now appears to be more radical and anti-Western ones, so that even the stability of a revolutionary government may serve American interests.

The second reason for the aid guideline is the importance of the continued independence of all existing Middle Eastern states, except as they may freely and voluntarily unite. Independence and the national pride which supports it are important barriers to the extension of Soviet or other foreign control which could threaten American interests. But the possible threat to independence arises less from the specter of direct Soviet military action than from the pressure inherent in the developmental process. In many Arab countries, especially in the radical ones dedicated to headlong change, the momentum toward improvement has become too strong to be checked. Promises have been too glowing, radical (and often beneficial) change too evident, to allow a government to stop its programs of progress. Since the necessary means to maintain and develop these programs often outstrip the resources of the country, foreign aid has been an essential which few governments can afford to relinquish without endangering their popular support. They need aid, but they want it without paying a price of subservience; hence their strident sensitivity to anything suggesting a political condition to an aid project. This feeling underlay President Nasser's outburst in 1965 when he angrily told the Americans to take their aid and "drink from the sea" because he had been (mis)informed that current aid negotiations had been broken off due to some of his government's actions.

With their commitment to nonalignment and dedication to national independence, many of the Arab states have striven to balance their aid between West and East so as to retain maximum freedom of action as well as to secure maximum help. But if one side sharply reduces or totally withdraws its aid, they may have no choice but to turn increasingly to the other, as happened in the U.A.R. with the ending of the American aid program in 1966. Thus the United States supplied aid to some Middle East countries so that they might not be pressed further into the Soviet embrace by the irrevocability of their developmental commitment. In this situation American aid was primarily designed to maintain independence, not to create a pro-Western or pro-American connection.

The third reason for separating aid from political and social systems is the desire of the United States to identify itself with the general cause of progress, which is espoused in movements and groups within the traditional countries as well as in the radical regimes of the revolutionary states. As has already been pointed out, opposing approaches to the means of modernization increasingly have divided the Arab world into hostile camps, which not only polarize political and economic systems, but also have opposing policies toward the outside world, including the United States. Because the traditional camp is, on the whole, more cooperative toward the United States, which has important specific interests in it (i.e., petroleum in the Arabian Peninsula and a strategic position in Iran), there could readily be an American policy especially favoring these states and backing their present rulers. Such a policy, however, would open America to the accusation that its interests lead it to be identified with the traditional system against which the awakened social conscience of the area is reacting. In contrast, the Soviets are often seen as having a freer hand and being heralds of change and of progress.

Groups seeking social change and radical innovation do not readily identify the United States with their cause. Western modes of development and American technology are highly respected and often desired in preference to Soviet patterns. Indeed, quiet talks with young leaders across the Arab world reveal that what they want for their countries is something like what the United States has rather than what Russia has. Yet they believe that what the United States has is not easily available to them because of America's commitment to its ex-colonial allies, to Israel, and to its own interests in the conservative states of the Arab world. Thus in 1958 President Nasser said in a public speech: "Russia has shown constant and sympathetic understanding of the fundamental needs of the United Arab Republic. The Five Year Plan of the Egyptian Province, the Ten Year Plan of the Syrian Province and that most vital and cherished of Egyptian projects, the Aswan High Dam, have all been granted support by the various Russian credit agreements." Earlier, in 1953, he forecast that this would be the case, for "the reason is simple: America is an ally of Great Britain, and both have a common enemy, Russia."

What President Nasser and most of his revolutionary colleagues in the Arab world would like is unstinting aid to their revolutionary cause by the United States. For reasons presently to be set forth, this is not in the American interest, but neither is it in the American interest to be identified exclusively with the traditional regimes and their slower, sometimes halfhearted, plans for progress. The alternative is to be identified with progress as such, regardless of the system under which it is being accomplished.

One more consideration supports the utility of the aid guideline. Thus far the argument has turned chiefly on the existing governments of the Arab world—their stability, independence, and desire for progress under different systems. But there are more than governments; there are people. To judge by the record of the last two decades, governments will continue to come and go, either violently or by more peaceful means, but the people will remain. Although in most Arab countries they cannot now express their attitudes through a democratic process, the weight of their opinion is a factor no leader can neglect entirely. Their opinion is not necessarily enthusiastically committed to the regimes which now hold power, either revolutionary or conservative. For the masses, the betterment of living conditions is still more important than political or ideological systems, as witness the Egyptian peasant's lack of enthusiasm for the Arab Socialist Union, his government's chief instrument for popular political participation.

A properly designed aid program is meant to reach beyond government and to have an impact on the common man. Here the American Food for Peace program has been especially effective. It touched the lives of large numbers of people in a simple, understandable form—food. American wheat and corn flour do not need to be identified by labels or the "clasped hands" trade mark; they look and taste different from the native product. Whatever may be the attitude of his government, the citizen who receives them knows that America is doing something for his welfare, and that knowledge may be an asset to American reputation and influence, especially if there is a radical change in regimes. The fact that a regime turned out of office was receiving American aid makes it possible for the succeeding regime to continue accepting the aid without being accused of being an instrument of American policy. The point was illustrated in Indonesia, where the cessation of aid in the closing months of Sukarno's supremacy made the new military group which took power from him cautious in accepting American assistance lest it appear that the United States was the motive force behind them.

Nonpartisanship in Local Disputes

The second guideline is that in quarrels between Middle Eastern states the United States will normally be nonpartisan. This can be called "American nonalignment" in Middle East disputes, the phrase having some utility as it applies to the Arab world. If Arab governments exercise their right to be nonaligned in global issues deeply affecting the United States, they should not object when the latter exercises the same right in their quarrels—even in one as serious as the Arab-Israel dispute. Few Arabs admit this, yet the logic is clear and has provided defensible grounds for retaining freedom of American diplomatic action.

As quarrels in the Middle East have increased in recent years, American diplomacy has generally followed the principle of nonpartisanship. Thus it did not take sides in the Greek-Turkish dispute over Cyprus, or in Pakistan's and India's clash over Kashmir. When the 1962 revolution broke out in Yemen, the United States recognized the new regime but did not back any of the three Arab states which supported opposing sides. It remained neutral in the Algerian-Moroccan border dispute in 1963. In the more difficult and involved Arab-Israel issue, official policy has been that of "equal and impartial friendship" toward both sides, as announced by Assistant Secretary of State Byroade in 1954, although few Arabs accept this as an accurate description of what the United States position actually has been, partly because America cannot by subsequent actions expunge from the record its role as a principal creator of Israel, partly because two decades of strident pro-Israel statements by political leaders (governors, mayors, congressmen, vice-presidents) overbalance the record of American action. The instantaneous anti-Americanism which swept the Arab world during the 1967 Arab-Israel conflict revealed how deeply the Arabs have been convinced that any American impartiality must stop short of the borders of Israel.

Several considerations have dictated the stance of impartiality. One is that the most vital interests of the United States in the area have not always been involved in an intra-area quarrel. When this is true, espousing the cause of one side against the other would increase American commitments beyond the necessary point of protecting American interest, while at the same time restricting the area of diplomatic maneuver. The clear lesson of recent years is that American commitments must be kept at a minimum and be undertaken only when the basic interests of the United States and world security are at stake. To take sides in the plethora of Middle Eastern quarrels, which will probably increase rather than diminish, would widen the responsibilities of the United States, place it under constant pressure to take drastic action, and unnecessarily increase the heavy demands on its military, diplomatic, and financial resources.

Moreover, the United States is not the only foreign power which could be drawn into a Middle Eastern dispute. The Soviets are a continuing presence in parts of the Arab world with interests of their own and a sympathetic clientele. If America espouses one side in an Arab quarrel there is the possibility that the Soviets will overtly support the other. Already the

U.S.S.R. has given various forms of assistance to anti-Western and anti-traditional movements when those serve their purposes. Given Soviet objectives in the area and the Arab penchant for seeking support from "the enemy of my enemy, who is my friend," this could well increase and become more effective, as the events of June 1967 showed.

It may be argued that since the American military position is so strong, the Soviets would make every effort to avoid challenging it. In support of this argument the Cuban crisis of 1962 can be cited. The citation is valid, yet the Cuban tactic cannot be often repeated. It is dangerous to assume that in every possibility of confrontation in the Middle East the Soviets will back down and let the United States have its way. Soviet interests in the Middle East are more important than they were in Cuba; the area is closer to the base of Soviet military power, and its potential influence in a strategic world position is much greater. American partisanship in Arab disputes, based on the expectation that the Soviets will always avoid trouble, would be a dangerous policy.

The possibility of a military confrontation arising out of a Middle Eastern dispute does not end the problem. Partisanship can be implemented in many ways short of armed action, as Viet Nam amply illustrates. Funds, arms supplies, technical advisers, aid projects, and diplomatic activity are also effective means of intervention. To a degree these have been and will continue to be used by both the Soviet Union and the United States in their competition for influence in the Arab world. But this competition is now general and takes place within the framework of normal relations (or "peaceful coexistence") between the two powers. If that competition comes to a focus in a specific case (such as the Arab-Israel quarrel) eliciting commitments on both sides to "credibility," it would sharpen tension between the Communist world and the United States, reduce the area for maneuver and negotiation for both, generate responsibilities not easily terminated, and further polarize the pro- and anti-Western attitudes in the Arab world. These results can be accepted with equanimity only if the question at stake so threatens American interests as to justify risking a major change in the American position in the area.

A further reason for this guideline is the ephemeral character of "friendship" in securing allies. It is sometimes argued that by supporting favored Arab states in disputes with their neighbors the United States would build up a circle of supporters on whose help it could rely consistently. There is little in the recent history of the Arab world to encourage this view. Since an Arab state, like all sovereign nations, acts under the dictates of its own interests, its interests do not and will not so continuously coincide with American interests that it can be counted upon as an unswerving ally.

Arab states which at one time have opposed the U.A.R. have, under their same regimes, assisted it at other times. It is an illusion to think that by supporting one side in Arab quarrels today America would win a permanent friend for tomorrow.

Some may object that the considerations given above take no account of any moral factor—the right or wrong involved in a Middle Eastern dispute. Leaving aside the profound and complicated question of morality and its place in the conduct of foreign affairs, the fact is that most Middle Eastern disputes do not present a situation in which the forces of light are clearly arrayed against the forces of darkness. If the United States were to take sides in the Turkish-Greek quarrel over Cyprus, or the Saudi Arabian-U.A.R. clash over Yemen, on the basis of a moral judgment as to where the ultimate rightness of the cause lay, it would show itself either to be hopelessly confused or naively misled.

Responses to Serious Threats

The first two guidelines may appear to emphasize unduly the limitations on the United States in the protection of its interests. More accurately, they propose the protection of American interests by separating them as far as possible from the turmoil of political and ideological strife in the Middle East. Although this appears to be the most productive course of daily diplomacy, it is not sufficient by itself to provide the full scope of American policy. A third guideline has therefore been developed. If a vital American interest is directly threatened, the United States will take direct measures to protect it. It makes no difference whether the threat comes from the radical or the traditional camp, from America's present friends or the presently not-so-friendly. If a threat emerges, a direct response will be given.

The response may take a variety of forms. In the last resort it could consist of military measures for the protection of a vital position, the safeguarding of an indispensable resource, or the prevention of outside or local aggression which would imperil American interests. But this would be a last resort, not to be used lightly or repeatedly. It runs the risk of increasing Soviet activity or abruptly terminating the American relation to Arab countries with damage to such interests as the United States may have in them. Unilateral military action is therefore most unlikely under present conditions, as American policy during the Arab-Israel clash showed. Yet its potential must remain, for by its very existence it helps prevent extreme and overt threats to the American position.

There are ways other than military action of responding to a serious threat. Diplomacy can sometimes be effective if the American interest is clearly and frankly placed before the government which contemplates threatening it, together with a warning of the seriousness with which the United States views the situation. Some diplomats hold that to do this is to weaken the American position by revealing its limits. It is better to keep a government guessing, they maintain, than to suggest the point to which it may go without risk of reprisal. Certainly no continuous and detailed review of all aspects of American policy can be shared with a Middle Eastern government. But the danger is that in a serious situation an Arab government may misread or misunderstand the nature of the American interest and the intention of taking a hard stand to defend it. Through miscalculation or inadvertence it may go beyond the point of no return, forcing the United States to take retaliatory measures which might have been averted.

One reason for the success of President Kennedy's dealings with

Arab leaders was the clarity and frankness with which he spoke and wrote to them, though always in a spirit of respect and equality. The American interests with which he dealt were clearly set forth, and Arab leaders felt that in so doing he was concerned to ease any possibility of inadvertent conflict. On more than one occasion in recent years, sober and quiet expressions of American concern have moderated a course which could have led to a serious breach between the United States and an Arab government. These expressions of concern were not delivered as ultimatums, but as reminders that there is a law of cause and effect in the world of foreign relations as well as in the world of nature. Given the character of a particular American interest, a challenge to it cannot help but generate a corresponding response.

That response might well involve actions at variance with the other guidelines of impartiality in aid and nonalignment in local quarrels. The consideration of the implements available to American diplomacy has made it clear that, short of military action, American resources for influencing the course of Arab policies are limited. At the crucial point, all these resources may be needed. Aid can be suspended, a country's opponents can be supported, and diplomatic pressure in the international community can be attempted. But this will be done only when a real and present danger to an American interest occurs, for this is the essence of the third guideline. It is the court of last resort when the situation is so serious that the United States is prepared to risk its position in the Arab world rather than relinquish the threatened interest.

The Basis for the Guidelines

Clearly the guidelines for policy formulation rest upon judgments as to the realities of the situation in the Middle East. They are "judgments" rather than "assumptions," for they derive from the actual record of developments rather than from theories about them. The judgments may be challenged, but the challenge must rest on facts which have been neglected or improperly appraised, not on dislike of the implications for foreign policy of the judgments as they now stand. If diplomacy is indeed the art of the possible, it must operate within a framework imposed by the facts of the situation. What are these facts, and what judgments are made on them to produce basic guidelines?

The first fact is that the postwar independence of Middle Eastern states has increasingly produced a variety of political and economic systems in the area, which differ, sometimes conflictingly, from state to state. The judgment is that this situation will continue rather than subside, and that no outside power has the resources either to reverse it or to impose a generally Western or generally Communist system on the area.

The second fact is that independence and the withdrawal of Western control have led to increasing disputes between Middle Eastern states. The judgment is that these disputes will continue to occur and that their resolution is in the hands of the governments of the Middle East rather than of any foreign power.

The third fact is that the Soviet position is a permanent element in the Middle East, at least for some years to come. The judgment is that despite restrictions which hamper Soviet as well as American action and the recession of danger from Soviet military threat, the U.S.S.R. will continue to be a competitor to the American position. It can be expected to exploit situations in which its support for indigenous movements and governments can embarrass the West.

The fourth fact is that the United States is restricted in its capacity to police or control the area. This is the result of the sovereignty of Middle Eastern states, the counterbalancing presence of the Soviets, the extent of American commitments elsewhere, and the nature of the implements available to American diplomacy. The judgment is that under these conditions the central concern of the United States must be to safeguard its most vital interests and not be drawn into commitments unrelated to them.

It must be emphasized again that the tactical guidelines which result from these judgments are not themselves policies. They are basic points of reference which have been used in formulating lines of action. The record of recent years shows that they have not been followed in every case. Divergence from them and inconsistencies within them are due in part to specific factors in specific situations, in part to the fact that in some cases the United States tends to react to a situation rather than act positively in it. But whatever the departures have been or may be, these basic points of reference will continue to influence the American approach to the Middle East until the facts of the situation change.

Chapter VI

Dilemmas

The American approach to the Arab world presented here has clear and persuasive reasons to support it. Yet for all the logic of the position, it involves dilemmas which have continuously and adversely affected the relations of the United States with Arab states. They have appeared partly in domestic American attitudes toward policies, partly in Arab reactions to them, and partly in the interruption of the pursuit of long-term objectives by the pressure of immediate and specific situations. These dilemmas cannot be brushed aside; they must be recognized and carefully weighed in assessing to what degree the approach of the recent past may be valid in the future.

The Wages of Impartiality and Nonpartisanship

The first dilemma is that impartiality in aid and nonpartisanship in regional quarrels necessarily has resulted in the United States supporting governments which cause it difficulty and systems of which many people disapprove. Most of the Arab states have at times taken actions or supported policies inimical to American interests or positions, both in the area and in other parts of the world. The nonalignment of some Arab states is so pro-Soviet that they have aided and abetted the chief rival of the United States in the Middle East. Pro-Western nonaligned states have not supported the American position in such matters as the Congo, Viet Nam, and nuclear testing. Where the United States has tried to secure stability and tranquility in the Middle East, some Arab states have persisted in actions which fan the flames of dispute—as the support of Jordan, Saudi Arabia, and the U.A.R. for the antagonists in the Yemen struggle. In the Arab-Israel dispute all Arab states have opposed the efforts of the United States to moderate the tension and resolve the situation peacefully. Even Lebanon, usually the most moderate and peaceful of Arab countries, felt forced to join in the Arab plans for diverting the Jordan River in 1964 and to recall its Ambassador from Washington when the Arab-Israel war broke out in 1967. Consistent compatibility with American interests and policies is a will-o'-the wisp in the relations of the United States with Arab countries.

None of the Arab states have political and economic systems in which the United States finds all the elements of a desirable democratic development. To varying degress the traditional monarchies are based on military power, a conservative elite which manipulates government for its own purposes, and a ruler with large personal power not effectively counterbalanced by a functioning parliamentary institution. Socially and economically all are seeking progress, but the pace is often hesitant, at least so far as rapid improvement in the lot of the masses is concerned. In the radical states progress is more rapid, but at the price of many personal and political freedoms and sound economic practices. The *ancien régime* with its privileged class and its quasi-democracy has been overturned, but the new order is moving toward a highly centralized state system under military control whose "democratic" institutions are at least as much a façade as those they replaced. Lebanon is the one truly republican government, which is, however, based on a delicate balance of religious groups, and has an uninhibited free enterprise system that lags far behind socially responsible practices in the West.

The United States is involved in this first dilemma to varying degrees in relations with all Arab countries. It comes to its focus and causes the gravest problems, however, in the support that has been given to the revolutionary states, of which the United

Arab Republic is chief. The catalogue of problems caused the United States by the U.A.R. is a long one. It was Egypt which first opened the doors of the Arab world to the Soviets and which has continued to give them their main base of influence. U.A.R. activities in Africa have included opposition to the United Nations action in the Congo and to the Leopoldville government (even to the extent of supplying some arms to the rebels), attempts to extend the Arab-Israel dispute to the Organization of African Unity, and covert support for a variety of African dissident movements. In the Arab world the U.A.R. has carried on an extensive program of vitriolic propaganda aimed at unsettling the conservative regimes, accompanied by a network or subversive activities through which Cairo keeps in touch with a wide range of Arab extremist movements. Its penchant for involvement in the affairs of neighbors has led it to post a huge occupying military force in the Yemen, causing one of the most serious Arab quarrels in recent years. In a speech attacking the American airbase in Libya, President Nasser precipitated a demand by the Libyan government that the base be removed. Many see in the U.A.R. the continuing center of Arab resistance to a peaceful solution of the Arab-Israel conflict and believe that it is Nasser's machinations which created the Arab-Israel conflict in June 1967.

The character of internal developments in the U.A.R. also has concerned many Americans. At the outset of the revolution there was much sympathy for the new regime, which appeared to be the long-awaited answer to Egypt's most serious internal problems. Its early record of land reform and the curtailment of the political power of the pasha class were accepted as the necessary prelude to a new and better society. But as the revolution continued, it developed in a direction which seems to be a combination of the fascist and socialist state. Even after a decade and a half, political power was tightly held by a small group supported by the army. No opposition party was allowed to form or express itself.

Courts became increasingly subservient to the political policies of the government. Sequestration of property and wealth affected many who by no definition could be considered enemies of the regime. Minority groups were under such pressure that large numbers of them fled the country. Individual citizens, especially of the upper class, periodically found themselves under surveillance. While not formally controlled, the press, in fact, was owned and directed by the government. Nationalization involved a considerable amount of foreign enterprise, for which adequate compensation was not promptly paid. Arab socialism may be difficult to define, but it represents a state-owned and controlled economy in which private enterprise has had little chance to develop. Such conditions may appear unavoidable to the Egyptian faced with the herculean task of building a new society in the ancient valley of the Nile. To the American they seem negations of many of the values he strives to uphold in the world.

Yet the guideline of aid without regard to the system of the host government has meant that the United States contributed to the support of regimes like that of President Nasser, despite their unpalatability and the problems they have caused. In a sense, the hand of American aid seemed to be pushing forward what the hand of American interest was pushing back. The result was that not only has American policy been accused of operating at cross purposes, but it has been continuously beset with opposition from domestic and foreign sources. By the summer of 1967, the accumulated American-U.A.R. differences, irrevocably capped by Nasser's action in setting the stage for an Arab war with Israel, were so great that no direct American aid program for building up the Arab world in the aftermath of war could be instituted if it included help to Nasser. Largely by its own actions, the U.A.R. had made the use of the "nonaligned" aid guideline impossible.

There has also been constant criticism from some of America's friends in and out of the Arab world. American aid given to the U.A.R. when that country was involved in a confrontation with Saudi Arabia over Yemen did not make sense to the Saudi government, which rightly considered itself among those having strong and friendly relations with the United States. The Egyptian nationalization of large Lebanese, Greek, and Turkish holdings without retaliatory action by the United States was bitterly, if privately, criticized by representatives of these countries. Iran, whose Shah has felt threatened by the revolutionary forces of the Arab world, did not understand why America contributed to their capacity to cause him trouble. Criticism of impartial aid in the Middle East has not been universal, but it has been exceedingly vocal, persistent and provocative.

Is there a way out of this dilemma? In simple terms the answer must be "No." Aid could be (and in some cases, has been) withdrawn from those countries causing the most problems, but the result has not increased the security of American interests. The course might engender momentary friendship among the Arab states opposing the revolutionary trend, but the assets they offer in support of the American position do not overbalance the loss of influence in the radical camp. The question the United States faces in many parts of the world can be phrased: Is it better to sever effective relations with difficult governments, surrendering them to their own radical nationalism with a preponderance of Soviet influence, or to maintain as good relations as possible with them for the sake of at least a minimum of influence and an opportunity for a continuing diplomatic dialogue?

Many critics of this aspect of the American position do not believe that it would be necessary to go the whole way in completely withdrawing support. They argue (as did the Lebanese, Greeks, and Turks when their property was sequestered) that the threat of aid withdrawal would have been sufficient to change the course of action. It has already been noted that this argument is based on exaggerated estimates of the size of American aid in most countries and the docility of a highly nationalistic government in paying the price of political conditions for an aid program, as well as on a misapprehension of the function of aid. The fact is that an aid program has rarely been used successfully for two different purposes at the same time. If its basic objectives are to assist stability and safeguard independence by providing an alternative to excessive dependence on the Soviets, it cannot at the same time be used as a bludgeon to force day-by-day changes in policy. To the extent to which aid has been used for overt diplomacy of pressure, its operations continuously affecting the uncertain course of the policies of the recipient government, it has ceased to be a dependable alternative to Soviet aid for that government or an asset to be counted upon in planning national development. Thus, pursuing the secondary objective may vitiate for the United States the primary object for which aid is given. In such circumstances the United States must choose which objective best serves its total interest and live with the problem this choice creates.

The dilemma, however, is not as sharp as it appears at first. No Arab government has been consistently hostile to the United States (except when the Arab-Israel issue is in the balance) or has always pursued policies at variance with American interests. Even those states which have caused the deepest misgivings have at times taken stands helpful to the American position. President Nasser raised the first Arab voice publicly and vigorously to protest the Soviet resumption of nuclear testing when he spoke before the conference of nonaligned states at Belgrade in 1961. He ceased supplying arms to the Congo rebels when it became apparent that they were losing the struggle and his relations with the United States were in jeopardy. Soviet attempts to obtain acceptance for the existence of Communist parties in the revolutionary Arab states have been consistently rebuffed, despite the presence of large Soviet aid programs. In general, the nonalignment of the radical Arab states has expressed itself in pendular oscillation between East and West rather than in maintaining a fixed position between the two. If the swing toward the Soviets has caused problems for the United States, the ensuing swing away from them has served American interests. The dilemma generated by so-called problem governments is thus not constant; it rises and falls with the frequently shifting and often unpredictable shifting actions of Arab states. If the American approach to the Middle East has seemed to support actions and systems inimical to American interests, it also and in the same state has supported others which have been helpful to them.

Moreover, those aspects of internal development in Arab

states which have been distasteful to Americans are not yet fixed in a permanent mold. In no Arab country—traditional or revolutionary—has the final shape of things to come emerged yet with unmistakable clarity. The traditional and revolutionary groups have their separate general direction of development, and in both camps there is a variety of forces at work. In most traditional countries there are groups striving for a more radical program of change; in the revolutionary states there are those seeking to temper the extremes of headlong policy. The stunning defeat of the Arab world at the hands of Israel has shaken its life to the core and provides a new setting in which almost anything can happen; more than ever, the path of the future is uncertain.

The situation has been strikingly illustrated outside the Arab world in the unexpected reversal of Sukarno's pro-Communist course in Indonesia. Opposition to that course was more widespread than foreign observers imagined; at the critical moment it gathered head and forced changes in policy that few would have predicted six months earlier. To a lesser degree the same thing happened in Algeria, where Ben Bella's extremes generated a moderating counteraction which swept him out of office. In hindsight it is clear that in both countries important centers of power were at variance with the course their governments were taking.

Thus it is wrong to assume that American assistance to a radical Arab government has supported monolithic systems, whose unpalatable features offer no prospect of change. The present prevailing atmosphere of a government in power may cause many misgivings and pose many problems, but the forces at work within the regime are too diverse and future developments too fluid to assume that changes cannot come. The dilemma does not involve a clear choice between systems which fall in with American ideas and those at variance with them. No system of government or economics in the Arab world has had all the elements Americans would like to see—and no system has been entirely without any of these elements. This does not resolve the dilemma, but it does moderate its tones, making clear that no Arab regime is all good or all bad from the standpoint of American interests.

The Status Quo

A second dilemma is that the United States has been cast in the role of a supporter of the *status quo* rather than as an active force influencing the course of events. Here *status quo* is used in its literal sense of the situation as it exists, not in the popular sense of a traditional, as opposed to a revolutionary, situation. The *status quo* in the Middle East involves a wide spectrum, running the gamut from the medievalism of parts of the Arabian peninsula to the radical socialism of the U.A.R. Strong-man army rule, constitutional monarchy, traditional Arab tribal leadership, and varying degrees of democracy are to be found in Arab governments. Economic systems have varied from the Lebantine brand of free enterprise to forms of state capitalism and socialism with or without Marxist hues. Methods for development and modernization range from the cautious and reluctant path of gradual evolutionary change to revolution and the overthrow of the old system and all its ways. In theory, since American aid has been available to all these differing forms as necessity and the protection of American interests may have required, the United States has appeared to be backing no particular pattern of political and economic development and to be seeking no special influence in shaping the future.

If the *status quo* in the Middle East were also a *status pacis*, this would not have caused so much difficulty. There is room for a multiplicity of systems to exist side by side. If varied systems to meet different conditions and problems existed in peaceful coexistence, the very diversity might enrich the area as it struggles to find new patterns to replace the old. But the *status quo* in the Middle East is not a state of peace; it is perilously close to a *status belli*—a state of war. Both the political ambitions of the independent Arab states and the different paths of modernization they tread have brought tension. In the opposition of the traditional to the revolutionary forces each camp is struggling not only for its own future, but for the future of the entire Arab world. Neither group has been notably successful in creating an enduring coalition to protect and further its position. Nasser's hope of building a revolutionary brotherhood whose "unity of purpose" would be expressed in unified action has had only intermittent and minimal success, while Feisal's Islamic Pact has been nebulous and uncertain. The very lack of permanent cohesion within the two camps has exacerbated their conflict as each state feels uncertain on whom it may count for support.

In the circumstances, the American position of not supporting one camp against the other, or one type of government and developmental system against its rival, has been open to two accusations. One is that American acceptance of the existing situation in the Arab world, with all its diversities, has been inconsistent with the interest of the United States in maintaining stability and tranquility. Insofar as the rivalries cause intra-area tension, they should be moderated or controlled where possible. Yet the United States does not appear to have undertaken this task, since its aid and political support was available to both camps. Once again it seems to have opopsed with one hand what it was seeking with the other.

The second charge is that the United States has abdicated responsibility for the emerging character of the new Arab world. What that character will be—revolutionary, socialist, army-controlled, or evolutionary with growing democratic institutions—may be the most important question for the future. Quarrels between neighboring states and the coalitions they generate will come and go and, with restraint, may be lived with; but the basic character of the emerging Arab world and the attitude toward competing ideologies will be an important factor in future years. If devolopments under way today can be encouraged in the path of moderate, constructive change within the framework of a growing democratic process, the new Middle East will be less of a threat to world peace, less likely to imperil basic Western interests, and more open to mutually profitable cooperation with the free world. By refraining from open and vigorous support of such developments and the countries in which they are occurring, the United States, it is alleged, has allowed other influences to flourish by default and has disclaimed a role in helping to determine what the future will be.

This dilemma is difficult for many to accept. Not only does the policy of noninvolvement appear to have been shortsighted in relation to the nature of American interest, but it has clashed with the feeling that the United States has both the duty and capacity to reshape the world—or at least those parts of it where it has important interests. For some Americans this feeling is a national commitment. It is galling to see a nation so predominant in world affairs and so vast in power and resources held at bay by small and newly independent states—whether in Viet Nam or in the Valley of the Nile. For others it takes on a moral character, the American equivalent of "the white man's burden." Since American democratic institutions and economic programs have provided one of the highest living standards in history, the United States has a mission to contribute its excellence to developing nations for their own good.

For those who would see the United States do more to keep order or to set the pattern of the future, the American stance of eschewing a vigorous active role in shaping the course of Middle East developments has aroused deep misgivings. Yet there is no ready escape from the dilemma. For one thing, it would be impossible at this stage for the United States to select a chosen instrument among the many governments and systems in the Middle East. No single Arab country or group has clearly established itself as the probable leader of the future. Although the U.A.R. will remain the largest polity there is no evidence to show that it can become the dominant power, swallowing up or controlling the major part of the Arab world. The short-lived union with Syria and the growing tension between the Yemeni republicans and their overpowering Egyptian partners point up the inherent difficulties the U.A.R. has had in its relations even with revolutionary Arab states. Nor are there any promising candidates for leadership in the traditional camp. King Feisal has shown himself a wise and progressive leader, and King Hussein has displayed bravery and skill in defending his country's position, but neither Saudi Arabia nor Jordan has given clear evidence of a capacity to lead the Arab world to its new day. The fact is that no clear pattern of present or future leadership can be identified, especially in the aftermath of the massive Arab defeat, and no present program of development or institution of government has proved itself to be the answer to the Arab world's needs. For the United States to choose to back one state or group of states and its leaders against others, in the hope that this will set forward a particular and triumphant course of development throughout the area, would be only an exercise in conjecture, not a sound judgment of reality.

The conservative, evolutionary approach of Jordan, Saudi Arabia, Morocco, and Libya has produced some sound and encouraging progress. But it has not demonstrated that it can deal effectively with the most basic social problems and the awakening expectations of the masses. These expectations will not be met merely by providing an increase in the gross national product under the leadership of an economic and political elite which uses more modern methods of production. What is demanded is as simple as Samuel Gompers' answer to the question what the objective of the newly organized American Federation of Labor was—"more." The demand is not only absolute for an increase in income and a rise of living standards; it is also relative. The middle and lower classes urgently press for a reallocation of national wealth to acquire a much larger share of the increment produced by modernization. In the latter days of monarchial Egypt, half the national income was absorbed by only 1.5 per cent of the population; the other half went to the remaining 98.5 per cent. Admittedly this was the situation at its worst, yet the evolutionary modernization going on in the traditional Arab states has nowhere shown that it can or will attack with vigor and success the problem of reallocating national wealth. Perhaps the present course of slow development is the best that can be expected in the countries following it, but few would claim that it is so successful that it can and should be the pattern for the future.

The revolutionary alternative to the traditional system has also failed to establish its program as the best pattern. To be sure, it dispossessed the wealthy elite, eradicated or curtailed landlordism, pushed rapid industrialization, and increased state services to the peasantry. In the opening years of revolution, rapid progress was not difficult to make as the more glaring failures of the *ancien régime* were attacked. Once the initial steps had been taken, however, the revolutionary regimes faced all the complexities of deep-rooted problems, ingrained attitudes, and basic economic reconstruction. Vigor was not lacking—but vigor is not enough to build a radical new system out of the ashes of the traditional past. Military leadership, on which most of the revolutionary regimes rely, may be dedicated, orderly, and more efficient than the *laissez-faire* civil service of the past; but its economic and political wisdom to design a stable, efficient pattern for the future has yet to be demonstrated, and its militant stance toward Israel has diverted badly needed resources from internal economic growth.

Many of the policies of revolutionary regimes have been highly pragmatic—which is to say that they have been more concerned with meeting immediate problems than with sustained progress toward a carefully selected goal. "Arab socialism" itself can best be understood as a pragmatic development, apparently born of the dissatisfaction of the Nasser regime with previous attempts to stimulate new industry, control the corruption of government by private entrepreneurs, and strengthen its own financial position. The nationalization of foreign and, later, Egyptian banks during and after the Suez crisis showed how easily a strong government can take over and profit from private enterprise. Government ownership and control of business and industry was then rapidly expanded, but without adequate planning for the problems of management and efficiency involved.

Thus it is not surprising that Arab socialism has varied from country to country. While having basic elements in common, the systems followed in Algeria, the U.A.R., Syria, and Iraq have been different. No single brand of Arab socialism has proved itself the regional pattern for development; and the accomplishments in the Arab countries which have adopted socialist systems have not yet demonstrated either its efficiency or its power to endure. The enthusiast for Arab socialism seen from afar (as in Libya or

Jordan) has often revised his opinion when he lived in its midst. For all the popularity it has mustered, Arab socialism has not proved that it is the wave of the future.

Two basic factors are involved in the failure of both the conservative and the radical camps to produce a convincing pattern for the Arab future. One is that the inherent diversities between the Arab states make it improbable, if not impossible, for a single political or economic system to fit the area as a whole. The tribal life of the Arabian peninsula, with its tradition of leadership by sheikhs and the multiplicity of its group loyalties, cannot be cast into the same rigid political mold as the agricultural, highly centralized life in the Valley of the Nile. The ratio of population to land and other natural resources varies widely. Egypt has nearly 30 million people penned in a narrow valley with not enough agricultural land to go around. Saudi Arabia has only some 4 million people scattered across a vast desert under whose sands lie some of the richest petroleum deposits in the world. No one system of development can encompass such diversities, and it seems inevitable that different paths of development will govern the future.

The second factor is the unsolved relation between private enterprise and state control in bringing about the rapid development needed and sought by all Arab countries. Private enterprise has a long history in the Middle East, creating what prosperity there was before the postwar period. Today it is the prevailing system of Saudi Arabia, Jordan, Lebanon, and Libya. While its record in these countries is encouraging, its more thoughtful proponents recognize that something additional is needed. Given the paucity of resources in many Arab states, the pressure for rapid development, the need for a larger share of wealth going to the masses, and the necessity of using more resources for national development and less for leisure-class luxuries, some participation by the state in economic planning and control is inevitable. A former Minister of Public Works and Chairman of the Middle East Airlines from Lebanon states the case as follows:

> Private enterprise ignored the pressing and urgent demands for social justice and did very little to improve the conditions of the masses either on its own or in cooperation with the public sector. . . .

Quite a change in our attitude toward planned economy has taken place during the last twenty years and our instinctive fear of planning as a "socialist-behavior" is growing less and less.

We are now ready to admit that a free economy and a certain portion of planned economy must co-exist and are necessary and even imperative for economic development. The extent of this co-existence in a developing country is quite different from that in a developed country. At the early stages of economic development planned economy may have to take an equal or even a more major part and then should [be] hand[ed] over partially or wholly to private enterprise and to free economy in the course of successful development.*

But just what mixture of state control and free enterprise will bring the most beneficial results in any one Arab country, much less in all of them, has not yet been found. In Lebanon it is free enterprise which is the dominant factor, in the United Arab Republic it is state control; but in neither have the results been so satisfactory that they can be taken as the prescription for other countries, or even as an adequate solution for their own problems.

Thus there has not appeared a single system or trend of development which the United States can uphold as either the likely winner in the race to the future, or the best candidate for directing its course. If it were certain that progressive traditionalism, based upon free enterprise, would become the prevailing system, American interests could be served by vigorously supporting and fostering it. If radical socialism were clearly the pattern of tomorrow, the United States might back it as the coming dominant force. But since neither has proved its case, an active role in fostering either and making it a cornerstone of policy would be to gamble American interests on a very uncertain future.

Activism vs. Passivity

It is here that the dilemma arises. Should the United States be content with a *laissez-faire* attitude toward the competing trends of political and economic development—a policy which has been

* *Congressional Record*, 89th Cong., 2d Sess., June 13, 1966, pp. A3159, A3160.

characterized as "don't do anything, just stand there"? Or should it throw its weight behind one system, in hopes of modifying it so that it may provide a sound answer to the needs of Arab development? In contemplating the latter course, two cautions must be sounded. One is that the American, for all his technical ability, has not shown that he has the capacity to design a new system which would answer adequately the needs of the Arab world. If Arab governments were to abdicate their responsibility for the shape of things to come and turn the task over to the United States, it is improbable that the result would be much better than any of the present systems. The same inhibiting factors would face the United States as now face Arab leaders, and the experience of Americans in their own affluent and democratic society is not readily applicable to conditions in many developing countries. Whatever solutions to Arab needs finally emerge, they will come from Arab leaders, economists, and planners who live within the situation and are aware of the limits of the possible. It may be that a long period of experiment and error awaits the Arab world before it discovers the best ways of reconstructing its life, but there is little possibility of shortening the process by attempts to impose a foreign-designed system, whether that system comes from the Communist camp or the West.

The other caution is that too close an identification of foreign backing with internal developments can be the kiss of death which prematurely ends a promising career. The intense nationalism of the Arab world, its sensitivity for newly acquired independence, its feeling that it has been too long a pawn of foreign interests, its schizophrenic fears of neocolonialism and its concern to be Arab as well as modern make sharp reactions against over-active foreign sponsorship inevitable. It is not that Arab leaders repudiate the institutions and methods of the modern world. They most desperately want them; but they want to make their own choices in the context of their own needs as they see them. Hence, "Arab" socialism—though not because there is an identifiable element of Arab theory or history in the system, most of whose features are drawn from European experience. It is "Arab" because the Arabs themselves selected the elements to meet their problems and to produce a system they can consider their own. An "American" system containing many of the same elements would be resisted.

No political or economic system which appeared to be foreign-inspired and strongly supported from without has much chance of success in the Arab world. This is one of the forces working against communism. As one Arab leader put it: "Despite our good relations with the Soviets, communism as a system is not for us. Its theory of the bourgeois class does not fit the Middle East. Its rigid economic prescription is not adaptable to our differing local needs and it always involves attempts at foreign control." An American-designed and sponsored political-economic pattern would be open to the same accusation.

Yet the dilemma is not as sharp as it appears, for the choice is not limited to complete indifference or active partisanship. Between these extremes lies an opportunity to encourage and foster diverse developments insofar as they effectively meet specific needs in the countries where they are found. This is in keeping with the American concern to be identified with change and progress wherever it may occur. Since there are both promising and questionable aspects of development in every Arab country, the United States could use a much greater degree of discrimination than it has in the past in selecting those which are most promising.

In general, two criteria should govern the selection. One is the economic effectiveness of the project or program, not in terms of the system in which it is embedded, but as demonstrated in its own concept and operation. It is not inimical either to American interests or the American system to assist varying types of development, provided the project is, or can be made, sound. The second test is whether the development is in the direction of a larger participation by the citizenry in political and economic activity. Again, the form of participation may not be in the pattern of American democratic institutions, but the principle of growing involvement of a people in their own welfare is one to which the United States is committed and which it believes can best serve the needs of developing countries.

These criteria are equally applicable to the traditional and the revolutionary systems. Under both, economic resources have been wasted by lack of adequate planning, failure to identify basic national needs, poor administration, and inability to curtail corruption. Under neither system has the potential of common participation in political and economic life been developed adequately. In governing its assistance by these two criteria the United States would be fostering a direction of development rather than a system of government or economics as such. Without attempting to dictate institutional forms, it would encourage trends within diverse systems, moving toward the same general goals, which are shared by groups in every country whose influence could be strengthened if the right kind of quiet support were given them.

If the United States is to do this, however, it must be willing to pay the price. Part of the cost is financial. It will take more than the limited aid of recent years to enable American influence to play a more decisive role in the development of the Middle East. Projects must be supported by grants or loans (even in countries with considerable resources of their own), more specialists made available, and a larger program for training national leaders instituted. Congress and American policy-makers must also develop a greater political maturity in sustaining programs through the fluctuations of current problems. The programming and direction of American aid will also need to undergo certain changes. Crash programs, fluctuating support, short-term projects, and indiscriminate support of national developmental budgets without regard to their economic soundness will not provide the United States with a favorable long-range identification. It is only a quiet, sustained, and dependable course of support for developments which meet its criteria that can enable the United States to influence the Arabs in their quest for a better future.

Moreover, Americans must be prepared for many frustrations and exercise greater patience and skill if they are to involve themselves successfully in this approach. Projects which touch the fundamentals of political and economic life are both sensitive and complex. Lack of experience and administration in host governments, a shortage of specialized, trained local leadership, and opposition from groups within their ranks make it difficult to move projects from promising initial stages to full integration into the nation's on-going efforts. The Middle East today is littered with projects which began well under American auspices but failed to take root permanently because they were not sustained through periods of difficulty. The notable success of private agencies like the Near East Foundation is due to their willingness to see a development start slowly, study and solve its problems within a limited area, then cautiously and with sustained support lasting as long as ten years move it to the national level under national leadership. Although the United States government has far greater resources for such purposes than any private agency, some drastic alterations in legislation, funding, and technique will be necessary if its aid is to be equally effective.

The dislocation of the life of the Arab world and the position of the United States in it which resulted from the June 1967 crisis brought the American aid program to a critical point. Arab development was interrupted, perhaps in some countries irretrievably set back, and new elements of political and economic instability appeared. At the same time, Arab resentment against the United States was so deep and universal that it may be a long time before a significant aid program can be reinstituted. A political settlement, or at least a *modus vivendi,* in the Arab-Israel dispute would appear to be necessary before any large and sustained American assistance to the Arab world can get underway. But when that time comes, there will be an opportunity freshly to approach the problem and it is then that American economic assistance policies can be reviewed, expanded and made more effective.

The Definition of American Interests

The need to protect American interests by direct action against direct threat poses a dilemma somewhat different in character. It is not so much a matter of restricted influence or contradictory actions as it is a question of definition and judgment. Great care must be used in identifying a situation in which the threat to an interest is sufficiently serious to warrant any form of direct action. If a commitment to action is made and is unsuccessful, or if the threat does not materialize, the United States runs the risk either of unnecessarily injuring its position without the compensation of a vital interest protected or of drawing back at the last moment and damaging the creditability of future commitments. This was the dilemma of Great Britain in the Suez crisis. By undertaking direct action the British laid in the balance their position in the Arab world. When the action proved ineffective that position was damaged irrevocably, without the British interest in maintaining international control of the canal having been achieved. Can the United States avoid similar situations by defining more clearly the circumstances under which it should protect its interests by direct measures?

Here there are three difficulties. The first is that while the general content of American interests can be stated, their specifics are more difficult to define. What constitutes reasonable Western access to petroleum, and in what situations would this be imperiled? The precise value the United States sets on such interests as oil is not constant; it changes with the general course of developments in the world and in the area. Middle Eastern petroleum remains essential to Western Europe, but the denying of Arab oil to Great Britain and the United States in 1967 did not precipitate the crisis it did in 1956. The interest in petroleum may now be more limited than it was ten years ago, thereby altering the situation in which the United States would be prepared to resort to direct action.

Moreover, with constantly changing conditions in the Middle East, the ways in which interests may be protected also change. When Egypt was at the crest of its influence in the Arab world and formed the United Arab Republic with Syria and the United Arab States with Yemen, some judged it to be a serious threat to the independence of other Arab countries. After 1962, although the U.A.R. remained the most influential state in the eastern Arab world, its deep difficulty in Yemen, the withdrawal of Syria from the union, the challenge of a coalition of conservative states under the leadership of Saudi Arabia, and its almost insoluble domestic problems had greatly altered its situation and capabilities. Any American interest involving Egypt must be reappraised in the light of these changes.

Such situations are illustrated by the changing position of Wheelus Field, the American air base in Libya. When the base rights were first granted, Libya had just stepped across the threshold of independence and welcomed the assurance of protection brought by the British and American presence. The rental paid for the base was a valuable addition to the Libyan economy, which was struggling with a paucity of resources. The royal family owed its position to British and American support and felt a community of interests with those powers. From the Western standpoint, Wheelus was an element of the defensive system to contain Soviet power since it provided air power near the southern perimeter of the U.S.S.R. and flanking Europe. Both for Libya and for the West, the British and American bases served mutual and vital interests which seemed to protect them against undue threat.

In 1963, however, a threat arose. In February of that year President Nasser publicly attacked the British and American installations in Libya as infringements on Arab independence. There was immediate reaction in Libya with a popular outcry demanding the removal of the bases. Only the drastic threat of abdication by King Idriss staved off the crisis, but both Britain and the United States found it possible, and indeed necessary, to agree to a review of the situation although the base rights still had some time to run. The days of Wheelus Field are now numbered, and the base will either be closed or greatly reduced in the future.

The change of attitude on the part of Libya and the United States resulted from the discovery of large petroleum resources in Libya, which made the rental paid for the base an insignificant part of the Libyan economy. The new national wealth more sharply divided the elite class from the common people—especially the new student and middle-class urban groups. The U.A.R.'s revolutionary program, carefully nurtured with propaganda, supported and fed growing dissatisfaction with the traditional order and made Arab socialism appealing to some of the more modern and radical elements. Nationalism is the inevitable concomitant of independence, and after twelve years Libya was less mindful of the help given by the West in achieving nationhood and more concerned with its status as an Arab state. As a result of these changes President Nasser's call fell on open ears, and Libya reacted against the presence of foreign bases in a way not predictable a few years ago. At the same time, the role of the bases had been changing. New types of weapons and their military strategies diminished the strategic importance of Wheelus Field. It became a staging facility to Africa and an all-weather training station for European-based air forces, important to NATO capabilities, but not in the front line of defense. When Libyan nationalism challenged the continuance of the base, and demanded its closure in the aftermath of the 1967 Arab-Israel war, it was possible for the United States to face withdrawal without irreparably damaging its defense interest.

The problem in the constantly changing definition of the specifics of American interests is two-fold: to keep definitions up to date and to secure general concurrence in them within the U.S. government. Too often American judgments on the Middle East are based on conditions which have passed or are passing. And too often they have lacked agreement of the community of agencies related to policy-making. When the Wheelus crisis arose, it was vital for the conduct of diplomacy to know precisely the importance the United States set on the base. Clearly, it was useful as a NATO adjunct, and its position on Arab soil could be an asset at a critical moment in Middle Eastern affairs. Did it then have such importance that the United States should consider going the whole way to protect it? At the time no satisfactory answer to this question could be obtained, partly because no current estimates were made available, partly because of differing estimates in the military and diplomatic communities.

The second difficulty lies in the relation, already mentioned, of American interests to American desiderata. The distinction must be stressed constantly. American policy-makers know better, but even some of them at times succumb to confusing interests with what are merely desirable developments. When the confusion goes beyond the policy-maker to Congress and the press, it generates pressures which make it difficult for an administration to keep American commitments limited to clear and present American interests. When this limitation is not maintained, the United States finds itself in the equivocal position that it did vis-à-vis Israel during the 1967 Arab-Israel confrontation. With Israel and the Arabs engaged in open hostilities, there was the expectation that the United States would honor its commitment to the defense and integrity of Israel, yet to have done so might have drawn the U.S.S.R. more deeply into the fray and led to an active Soviet-American confrontation. American interests demanded that this be avoided, but the American commitment, taken at face value, might have brought it about. Quite properly the United States chose its interests over its commitment—yet this situation would not have arisen had interests and commitments been kept in balance.

More difficult is that nebulous zone between interests and desiderata in which the problems of the future may be found. If it could be foreseen that the present course of an Arab state or its leader was moving toward a certain threat to American interests in the future, it could be argued that preventive action should be taken now before the threat occurs. In effect, this would call for some form of American response (military, economic or diplomatic) although no immediate threat to an interest exists.

Opinions on the wisdom and effectiveness of such a course differ widely. If the analysis made in this study is sound, it indicates that many situations in the Middle East are too fluid to predict. Many possible future threats to the American position have been envisioned. Nasser's ambitions in his heyday could reach to the oil fields at the head of the Persian Gulf; the proposed Islamic pact could lead to a revolutionary-traditional conflict among the Arab states; the Soviet position in the U.A.R. and Syria could be so strengthened that the two countries would approach a satellite status. But for every fearful possibility there is also a hopeful one. Egyptian attempts to create and control a permanent revolutionary following have not been successful, and its military capacity proved illusory. A period of sharper tension between the traditionalists and the revolutionaries may well be in the offing, but neither the U.A.R. nor Saudi Arabia has demonstrated a capacity to form permanent coalitions which can outlast the shifting alignments within the Arab world. The Soviet position causes concern, but Russian attempts to move to a point where it can completely dominate policy in the U.A.R. and Syria thus far have been thwarted by the force of nationalism. Nowhere is it more true than in the Middle East that "if hopes be dupes, fears may be liars." To precipitate a crisis in the expectation that a future threat will be headed off demands a gift of prophecy that American (and other) policy-makers have seldom displayed. Yet the question will continue to arise, posing the dilemma of acting now or waiting until the crisis has come.

The third difficulty in the definition of American interests is related to the problem of contingency planning. Constant preoccupation with current conditions can too easily deflect the policy-maker from considering what shape of American interests and the form of their protection in the future may be. At the moment there is a close connection between the American interest in petroleum and the regimes controlling the oil-producing states. For most of them there appears to be no immediate substitute leadership which could take over political power, give stability to the country, and lead it in a new direction without interrupting the flow of oil. American interest at the present time, therefore, seems to involve support for the existing regimes, despite some of their distasteful characteristics and continuing problems. This leads to the conclusion that some form of direct action might be necessary to support the regimes if they face a critical threat. It is partly on this basis that the United States sought to confine the Yemen struggle to Yemen, fearing that if it spilled over into Saudi Arabia it could threaten the continuance of royal rule and bring dangerous instability to the country.

But what is to be done if these regimes are threatened by forces to which the United States cannot or will not make a direct response? It is one thing to defend a government from foreign pressure; it is quite different to save it from internal discontent, especially if a revolt breaks out in the name of modernity and progress. Are the interests of the United States so bound up with the rule of regimes that all is lost if they disappear? Or must the contingency of their disappearance be taken into account for a policy which looks beyond the present to alternate actions in a radically different future?

Contingency planning is both difficult and inconclusive. It deals with situations not yet in being and proposes solutions which at best can be little more than hypotheses. Situations seldom occur in the specific form predicted for them, and the range and effectiveness of American future action are conditioned by factors which do not appear fully until the crisis is at hand. Like its military counterpart, political contingency planning is an exercise in analysis. It can identify factors which must be taken into account in future decisions and work out theoretical responses to assumed conditions. Rarely can it result in a detailed policy, which can be taken out of the file and put into action as needed. Its value lies chiefly in the development of a tested and familiar process by which situations can be analyzed when they occur, and the alternatives of American action identified and weighed.

One of the most inescapable attributes of the diplomat and policy-maker is preoccupation with the kaleidoscope of daily events and immediate problems. These are the substance of their pressing responsibilities and it is easy to become so immersed in them that there is neither time nor vision to look into the future. Yet the future not only has problems which should be prepared for now, but its possibilities affect judgments on current situations. Sustained contingency planning counteracts this absorption in the present and adds a dimension of range and flexibility which American policy needs. But it does not predict accurately what will happen and what should be done about it.

If the tactical guidelines have resulted in such serious dilemmas, why were they followed? The answer is that the alternatives containing fewer or less inhibiting problems did not appear. In some form these dilemmas have been incident to American policy from the beginning of its active role in the Middle East. They did not arise so much from a policy choice as from the nature of the situation in the Middle East and the limits of American capabilities. Future policies probably cannot avoid them; they must be lived with as part of the price for undertaking responsibilities in Middle Eastern affairs.

Chapter VII

Yemen—A Case Study

The civil war in Yemen which broke out in 1962 confronted the United States with a most vexing problem in its recent dealings with Arab affairs. What appeared at first to be only an internal dispute in a remote corner of the Middle East unexpectedly expanded to involve two major Arab states in protracted confrontation. British difficulties in the neighboring Colony and Protectorates of Aden were multiplied and complicated, and the possible range of Soviet activities in the region was increased. A military-political impasse was created in Yemen from which there was no simple way out. Here in microcosm were most of the elements and difficulties involved in the American approach to Arab affairs. The diplomatic response to this situation was within the framework of the current guidelines and resulted in the dilemmas incident to them.

American policy in Yemen has been sharply criticized. Domestically it has been attacked by members of the petroleum industry operating in the Middle East, by pro-Israeli groups including congressmen and columnists, by those who for diverse reasons oppose any American action which appears to assist the U.A.R., and even by some in government agencies related to foreign affairs. Great Britain, especially the British Colonial Office, was unhappy with the American position, and the Arab states involved have, at the least, been uncomprehending of the *raison d'être* of American actions. Accusations have been made that the United States, in fact if not in intent, supported Egyptian aggression, opened the door to expanded Communist influence in the Arab world and increased the threat to the British position in Aden. The situation in Yemen was obscured by a fog of propaganda, the royalists with funds from Saudi Arabia being especially active in the United States. Through the mists it was difficult at times to ascertain the true state of affairs and to keep the eye of the policy-maker, and of his critics, on the fundamental question: "What are the interests of the United States in Yemen, and in what sense are they being threatened?"

The Background to Revolt

Yemen is remote from the main currents of the Arab world and even more remote from direct American interests. It is a small country (74,000 square miles), situated in the southwest corner of the Arabian peninsula with a coastline on the Red Sea. Its estimated population of 4.5 million is divided between the town dwellers (principally in Taiz, Sana and Hodeida) and the much larger tribal group who live mainly in the mountainous area. The country is split by religious difference, 40 per cent of the people, chiefly in the highlands, being Zaidis (one of the Shia sects of Islam); the remaining 60 per cent are Sunnis, the faith of most of the Muslim world, including adjacent Saudi Arabia. Traditionally, the elite class controlling government and leading the tribes has been Zaidi.

Until the recent revolution, Yemen was a theocratic autocracy with power centered in the personal rule of the Imam, supported by his religious character as well as by his political power. But neither the religious nor political authority was unquestioned. The Sunni majority did not accept the religious role of the imamate and the tribes only bowed to political control when the Imam had enough power to enforce his writ or enough skill to play one tribe against the other to his own advantage.

Since the end of the Second World War, this Tibet of the Arab world has been more influenced by the currents of modern life.

Large numbers of Yemenis (an estimated 50,000–75,000) have served in the labor force of neighboring Aden, where they absorbed European ideas and experienced a material richness of life unknown in the austerities of their homeland. Some students went abroad to study, chiefly in the surrounding Arab countries but with a few coming to Europe and the United States. As a result of these contacts with modernity, dissatisfaction with the backwardness of the country began to appear. In 1948 and again in 1955 there were revolts. In the first, the Imam was murdered, but a few weeks later the Crown Prince routed the rebels and assumed rule. In 1955 Imam Ahmad was forced to abdicate briefly by one of his sons, but the plot failed and Ahmad resumed the throne. It may seem that such attempts were little more than family struggles for power within the establishment, but beneath them was growing unrest which warned that things could not remain as they were in Yemen.

In 1962 there was one more revolt in the Yemen. Yet it was not simply "one more," for it was different in character and effect from any previous political movement. It was not led by a member of the royal family seeking the throne for himself, but by a professional soldier; its object was the abolition of the imamate as a governing institution. Its impact was not confined to Yemen but spread to embroil Saudi Arabia, Jordan, and the United Arab Republic, and finally to engage the attention of the United Nations. After five years of fighting, two governments claiming to represent Yemen still existed and the resolution of the situation seemed as distant as ever.

On September 19, 1962, the Sana radio announced the death of the aging Imam Ahmad and the accession of his son, al Badr. A week later Brigadier Abdulla al Sallal, commander in chief of the small Yemeni army of 18,000 men and commander of the Imam's bodyguard, led a swift coup d'état in Sana which proclaimed Yemen a republic, ending ten centuries of the imamate, and announced a program of political and social reform. But the Imam, who was reportedly killed, escaped with other members of his family to the north and rallied some of the tribes to his cause. Initially the new regime had control of a major part of the country. Many tribal leaders remembered the executions of their relatives by Imam Ahmad and either supported, or were neutral toward, the al Sallal government. But as guerrilla fighting spread and the new regime sought to extend effective sovereignty through the highlands, tribal loyalties began to oscillate between the royalists and republicans, depending on how the struggle went, who displayed present power, and how generous and frequent the subsidies were. What appeared at the beginning to be an accomplished fact of country-wide success gradually became only a firm acceptance of the regime in the towns and the regions about them, with neutral or hostile tribes controlling the highland desert areas.

Arab Intervention and Confrontation

What moved this struggle from a domestic affair (as in the revolts of the past) to an Arab world problem was the involvement of Saudi Arabia, Jordan, and the United Arab Republic as supporters of the royalist and republican forces. The involvement of the U.A.R. was not unnatural, for Yemen had a history of friendly relations with Egypt. After the formation of the Arab League in 1945, Yemen almost invariably was in the Egyptian "bloc," as opposed to the Iraqi and neutral "blocs." In 1956 it entered into a joint security treaty with Egypt and Saudi Arabia, and after the union of Egypt and Syria in 1958, it associated itself with the new country through the formation of the United Arab States. Thus there was already a continuing political association between Yemen and Egypt and it was natural for al Sallal to turn to Cairo for support in his revolutionary effort. Whether he attempted to invoke the memory or the spirit of the security pact is not clear, although at the time the U.A.R. government indicated that this was a factor in its response. More important was the revolutionary character of the republicans' objectives. While not taken in detail from the Egyptian system, they looked in the same direction, being based on the conviction that only a radical reshaping of society could accomplish reform and modernization. The appeal for Egyptian help thus had two arguments to support it: a history of Yemen-Egyptian political relations, including a defense undertaking; and the assistance of a sister revolution against a regime which even many Arabs considered medieval and outmoded.

The U.A.R. was not slow to respond. After three days of consideration, the decision was taken to support the republicans in their struggle. Trainers, advisers and military equipment were dispatched to aid the small Yemen army. But what began on a modest scale quickly escalated to involve an Egyptian expeditionary force, which at its height may have numbered as many as 70,000 troops. Egyptian soldiers fought actively in the field, Egyptian fliers in Russian planes carried the brunt of the bombing, and Egyptian administrators controlled the government. In the end there was an Egyptian occupation of the country without which the republican regime would have collapsed.

Why did the U.A.R. embark so blithely on what has turned out to be a frustrating and costly adventure? Some claim it was part of a Nasser blueprint for conquest—a deliberately planned step in a strategy to expand Egyptian political control over the Arab world. There is little evidence to support this view or to indicate that the U.A.R. directed the coup d'état. The revolt arose from natural causes within Yemen, not from Egyptian machinations. It had been the policy of the U.A.R. to keep in touch with many dissident movements in the Middle East and to make use of them when and if they might serve a national interest. There had been several Free Yemeni groups in Cairo with which the Egyptian government had continuing contacts. There is some reason to think that revolutionary groups both within and outside Yemen may have expected Egyptian support if they mounted a potentially successful coup d'état. Yet the decision to enter the Yemen struggle was largely a pragmatic one, made at the time of the revolt and in the light of its particular character.

Subsequent events show that the U.A.R. was unprepared for what its involvement in the Yemen brought. At the outset it knew little about the country and less about the vagaries of tribal life and its fleeting loyalties. It did not foresee the depth of involvement to which it had become committed or the size of the military support it would need to supply. The shifting tactics of guerrilla warfare, of which the Arab tribesman is past master, baffled the Egyptian army.

There were several reasons why the U.A.R. entered the Yemen dispute so quickly. It is significant that the Yemen revolt occurred a few days short of a year after Syria broke up the original U.A.R. and turned its back on Nasser. In the aftermath of disunion, Egypt was considered by Arab neighbors to have reached the nadir of its influence and failure to respond to al Sallal's appeal would have confirmed that impression. The Egyptian action was thus partly an affirmation that the truncated U.A.R. and its leader were still strong and to be taken into account in Arab affairs.

Moreover, the republican appeal invoked loyalty to the re-volutionary cause. Revolutionary movements frequently generate a missionary dedication and Egypt, as the largest Arab state, be-lieved it had an obligation to assist fellow Arabs who chose the revolutionary path. Whatever the temporal suitability of the imamate system to the medieval outlook of Yemen, few Arabs saw hope of progress under the Imam's leadership. The appeal of the Yemeni republicans, who stood for radical change, was directed to a regime and a leader who by nature and instinct were activist, tending to respond to any call for help which involved their prestige and revolutionary dedication. Thus the decision to enter the Yemen affair appears to have been based largely on pride and principle rather than on a carefully calculated estimate of the situation and its relation to Egyptian national interests.

Saudi Arabia and Jordan entered the Yemen struggle shortly after the U.A.R. recognized the al Sallal government. Their de-cision was due in part to an instinctive reaction against Egyptian activism. For some years, and especially since 1958 when Syria and Egypt united to form the United Arab Republic and the Kassim revolt in Baghdad destroyed the sister Hashimite throne and led Iraq into the revolutionary camp, Jordan had found itself partially surrounded by revolutionary regimes in which Egypt and President Nasser played a leading role. King Hussein's fear of subversion and intervention from outside was heightened by the discontent of his ex-Palestinian subjects, who made up some two-thirds of Jordan's population. When Syria separated from Egypt in 1961, Jordan recognized the new Syrian government within a few hours, and Egypt then immediately broke diplomatic relations with Jordan. Thus Jordan was naturally suspicious of Nasser's intentions in Yemen and saw his moves there as Egyptian imperialism.

The Jordanian monarchy also saw revolt in the Yemen as a serious threat to its own existence. The generally slow progress of modernization, alleged willingness of the Hashimite dynasty to consider coming to terms with Israel, the support tendered the throne by the British and American "imperialists" and the desire of the ex-Palestinians to regain the whole of Palestine created continual internal discontent and demands for radical change. If in the name of modernization and progress a traditional government in Yemen could be overthrown, the infection might spread to Jordan and spark revolt there. King Hussein felt that he had a stake in the triumph of the Imam and his cause and undertook to assist the royalists through a supply of arms and training missions.

That the move was not universally popular in Jordan was evident when the commander of the Jordan Air Force and two pilots defected to Cairo, raising the question of how heavily the royal regime could count upon the loyalty of its army. Some of the King's political advisers and supporters felt that the country did not have either the resources or the internal stability to risk mounting a foreign intervention—especially to combat a cause opposed to traditionalism. Yet Hussein's action was natural for a regime which found itself threatened by revolutionary discontent from within and the target of revolutionary appeal from without.

Similar factors operated to draw Saudi Arabia into the struggle. While relations with the revolutionary regime in Egypt had been reasonably cordial at the outset, they worsened as Nasser attempted to extend his leadership into the Arab world. The growing relations between the Egyptian regime and the Soviet bloc worried the Saudis, whose strongly traditional religious outlook and government ardently opposed "godless communism" as the antithesis of Islam. Moreover, the petroleum industry, on which the wealth and possibility of progress in Saudi Arabia were entirely dependent, made cooperative relations with the West a necessity. Any move in the Arab world which might jeopardize this relation or place the oil resources within the sphere of Soviet influence and control aroused deep, if sometimes concealed, opposition.

Both the formation and the dissolution of the Syrian-Egyptian union played on these fears. In forming the union in 1958, Nasser appeared to have taken a first and effective step toward dominance over the surrounding Arab states. Conservative neighboring regimes could not help but worry about "who will be next," and Saudi Arabia took no pains to conceal its rejoicing when the union was dissolved in 1961. As in the case of Jordan, this reaction struck at President Nasser in his most vulnerable and gloomy hour and resulted in strained relations, although diplomatic representation was continued. Moreover, Egypt emerged from the ruptured union more firmly and publicly committed to a radical and (in Saudi eyes) pro-Communist course. President Nasser stated that the basic cause for the rupture was Syrian failure to accept and follow the revolutionary program and that henceforth the reconstituted U.A.R. could have close relations only with those states which shared its revolutionary goals—the policy of "unity of purpose." The goals became more explicit with the nationalization of Egyptian industry in the summer of 1961 and the ensuing development of Arab socialism. To Islamic, free-enterprise, monarchial Arabia, this seemed like a brand of, or entering wedge for, communism, and Egypt was increasingly viewed as a willing or unwitting tool for Soviet-Communist designs on the Arab world. As the Saudis saw it, Nasser's decision to intervene in Yemen brought this threat onto the soil of the Arabian peninsula. An immediate reaction was predictable.

The reaction was sharpened by the situation within Saudi Arabia itself. The impact of the petroleum industry had brought the twentieth century, with all its developments and temptations, into the heartland of Arabia and created a new group of modern-minded Arab technicians and entrepreneurs. Huge oil royalties offered a potential for progress and modernization to meet the awakened expectations of this new group, but they were administered by the government of a conservative and traditional society. The founder of the kingdom of Saudi Arabia, the great Abd al Aziz Ibn Saud, had shown remarkable skill in shepherding his people from medievalism to the beginnings of modernity, but with his death in 1953 the throne passed to his son Saud Ibn Saud, who had little of his father's ability. During his rule there was growing discontent among the leadership class, and as an institution the royal family suffered in reputation and effectiveness. By the time civil war broke out in Yemen the king had reached the nadir of his influence and had reason to worry lest revolution against a traditional throne in a neighboring country might ignite a movement against him at home. That these fears were not groundless was shown by the defection of seven Saudi air force pilots to Cairo two months after the al Sallal coup d'état. It is reported that the king had the storage batteries removed from the tanks of the Royal Guard in Riadh lest they be turned against him.

To self-preservation was added the instinct to support a fellow monarch. Even though the ruling family in Yemen was Zaidi and not Sunni, and was recognized as limited and medieval in its outlook, King Saud did not think his interests would be served by the disappearance of another king. He therefore gave the Yemeni royal family refuge within his borders, supplied large sums of money to buy tribal loyalties and modern weapons, arranged for the stockpiling of military supplies on Saudi soil at points close to the Yemen borders, and together with Jordan provided military officers to teach the tribesmen how to use modern arms. Since Saudi Arabia had no lack of money, its assistance to the royalists could be large and sustained, in contrast to Jordan's modest effort.

Opinion throughout the Arab world was divided and inconclusive. Many feared Egyptian expansion and the extension of President Nasser's activities. At the same time, few had any good words to say for the imamate as a system or its record in meeting the needs of Yemen. Under King Saud, Saudi Arabia had lost the reputation acquired for it by his father and was looked upon as a government whose wealthy and numerous royal family were more interested in spending the oil royalties for their own pleasure than in bringing about progress. The dominant size and military capacity of Egypt made it difficult for any Arab state openly to oppose U.A.R. policy in Yemen; the character of the imamate and the Saudi monarchy made it equally difficult to support them in the struggle.

The American Interest

The purpose of this chapter is not to pursue the developments and vagaries of the continuing struggle in Yemen, but to determine how the United States acted in this situation and why it took the course it did.

What were the American interests involved in strife in Yemen? The answer was complicated by the fact that the administration did not state identical objectives to the various audiences it addressed. Congress and the press were under the impression that getting the U.A.R. out of Yemen and curtailing Nasser's foreign adventures were major concerns, while within diplomatic circles the emphasis was on confining the Yemen conflict to Yemen. In the limited sense of "interests" as used in this study, the United States had none in Yemen per se, although it could not help but be concerned about a situation which might imperil the stability of surrounding areas. There was little American investment in or trade with the country; one American concern had explored for oil but left after drilling a series of dry holes. It made little difference to the American position whether Yemen was ruled by an imam or a president, by Nasser, the Saudis or the British. Civil war in Yemen or an Egyptian occupation would not in themselves evoke a significant American response.

But there were American interests outside Yemen which could be affected by the outbreak of civil strife within that country. One of these concerned the petroleum resources at the head of the Persian Gulf—a basic and continuing interest of the United States. While in its most technical sense this interest concerned the accessibility and security of petroleum resources, it also involved a cordial and continuing relation with the kingdom of Saudi Arabia. It was under American engineers that the Saudi oil fields had been explored and developed, and American oil companies have played an important role in assisting in the modernization of the country. At a crucial period in Arab-American affairs, the crown prince of Saudi Arabia referred to the American oil companies as his country's "partners" in its national development. This description is a valid reflection of the general American relation to Saudi Arabia, based upon a mutual concern for the development and utilization of its petroleum wealth. The American interest in oil was thus embedded in a concern for the stability and progress of the Saudi government and people.

Fighting in Yemen did not threaten Saudi Arabia and the oil fields directly, nor did the Egyptian expeditionary force appear to have either the objective or the capability of attacking them. As a platform from which to mount an invasion of Saudi Arabia or drive toward the control of the oil area, Yemen has little potential, for it is distant from the centers of Saudi life and even more distant from the oil fields. Between them stretches an arid and inhospitable desert which could swallow up an army as easily as the western desert in Egypt engulfed the Persian expeditionary force against Libya in the sixth century B.C. Thus it was not the threat of military action which activated American diplomacy.

But revolt in Yemen and the Egyptian-Saudi confrontation which it quickly generated might nonetheless have imperiled the continued stability of Saudi Arabia. The danger lay in the possibility that the conflict would so shake the existing government that it would lose control or possibly be overturned by revolt. In the resulting chaos, the petroleum resources, so important to both the United States and the Saudis, could be threatened or at least temporarily affected. This possibility touched American interests at a vital point.

The Yemeni conflict threatened Saudi stability in three ways. If the Egyptian-Saudi confrontation became too sharp and prolonged, the Egyptians might be tempted to start open hostilities, invade Saudi soil, and involve the kingdom in a war which would tax its political, if not its financial, resources. Or discontented factions within Saudi Arabia, either by themselves or aided from without, might attempt revolutionary action to replace a moribund royal regime with a system more to their taste. A third possibility was that the strain of intervening in Yemen, not fully popular with many Saudis (especially at the outset), in a situation where a reasonably quick and conclusive royal victory was highly improbable, would erode the position of the already unpopular king to the point where he would lose control of the country. No political group in Saudi Arabia could be identified as a dependable replacement for the existing regime, so that the American interest involved supporting that regime despite its questionable stability. Whether Egyptian troops came or went was in itself not the vital question.

The second American interest also involved stability—this time in Jordan, even more remote from Yemen than the oil fields. As the inheritor of part of the territory of former Palestine, Jordan was in a sense an Arab counterbalance to Israel. Jordan's tenuous stability has repeatedly been shaken by the discontent of some of its former Palestinian citizens and its recurrent clashes with the revolutionary regimes of neighboring states. The pro-revolution, pro-Arab unity, pro-Nasser element is much stronger in Jordan than in Saudi Arabia and could respond with open enthusiasm to revolt in Yemen, which appeared to be both a triumph for radical reform and an extension of Egyptian leadership. Jordan had no borders contiguous with Yemen and there was no danger that Egyptian or republican Yemeni military action might threaten the territorial integrity of the country. What was threatened was the uneasy equilibrium of the monarchy, which, if destroyed, could have led to a move for union with or domination by the U.A.R. Should this occur there was serious risk that Israel might respond with military action.

Thus the object of American diplomacy was to create a situation in which the integrity and stability of Saudi Arabia and Jordan would be protected from the shock waves of civil war in Yemen. By entering the fray on behalf of the royalist cause, the two countries were committing their resources to a prolonged and uncertain struggle and inviting an ever sharper Egyptian response. Given this involvement, the question the United States faced was how civil war in Yemen could be confined to Yemen and defused as a threat to neighboring countries.

Recognition

The response to this question cannot be understood without appreciating the character and style of the Kennedy administration. By nature and commitment, the President was an activist, envisioning a "new frontier" of American influence abroad as well as in domestic progress. During the election campaign he had repeatedly attacked the fading reputation of the United States in world affairs and the aura of inconclusiveness surrounding the American image abroad. As president, he took vigorous leadership in formulating foreign policy, giving special attention to situations in which he felt that American policy had been too long at dead center. This was reflected in some of his ambassadorial appointments, where he selected men with special knowledge of and experience in countries where American policy had seemingly resigned itself to the inevitable.

Yet the activism of the new administration was not expressed by adopting hardline policies as the implement for increasing American prestige. The President's early meeting with Khrushchev and the debacle of the Cuban invasion in April 1961 were warnings that tough talk and tough tactics were not the invariable ingredients for success. While the confrontation with the Soviets over Cuba in October 1962 showed that the administration was prepared to go to the limit when basic American security was threatened, it was clearly not a policy which could be repeated frequently. Another approach was needed and the President therefore adopted an active policy of diplomatic intercourse, dialogue, and persuasion to seek his ends. This was true even in the Cuban affair, where military confrontation was not pushed past the point where the immediate threat to American security had been stopped.

In the Middle East, the new diplomacy took the form of attempting to develop an influential, mediating role in which

American prestige and judicious pressure would be used to open ways of escape from some of the area's impasses. The President's frequent and personal correspondence with Arab chiefs of state was one expression of this approach. His letters were clear and substantive, speaking to current issues and stating the American position with frankness. Yet they were never condescending or peremptory. To an unusual degree, President Kennedy was sensitive to the political problems faced by Arab leaders and took these into account in his dealings with them. A consummate politician, he understood the necessity of dealing with the reality of other people's situations, using discussion, persuasion, and the search for mutual interests to keep a question open until it could be moved toward some resolution.

The outbreak of strife in Yemen confronted the new administration with its first major crisis in the Middle East. The separation of Syria from Egypt in the fall of 1961 had not raised serious policy questions since it did not imperil American interests or threaten to disturb the stability of neighboring Arab states. The Arab-Israel problem has been the burdensome heritage of every new administration, but its general form had long since been determined by the decisions of earlier policy-makers, the pressure of special groups in the United States, and the inexorable flow of nearly two decades of history. But the Yemen situation brought unexpected new tensions between important Arab states where the United States had special interests. The administration reacted promptly and vigorously to a challenging opportunity to utilize the new diplomacy and to play a positive, rather than an acquiescent, role in Arab affairs.

The first question to be faced was that of extending recognition to the republican regime. In hindsight, many critics charge that recognition was given precipitously, without adequate justification in the factual situation of the time, and in neglect of a careful consideration of the consequences. In American policy, recognition has usually contained a political as well as a factual element. Given the situation during the opening months of the Yemen struggle and the American objectives, recognition was considered partially as a tool for diplomacy in protecting American interests. It must be noted that the United States did not rush in to accept a new government in Yemen out-of-hand. The coup d'état occurred on September 27; not until nearly three months later was recognition extended to the Republic of Yemen. During these months the republican cause had won the support of the chief centers of Yemeni political life (the urban areas) and controlled a significant part of the country as a whole. The royal family had fled to Saudi Arabia, and tribal opposition was largely confined to the arid, mountainous border regions. These had never been fully controlled by any Yemeni ruler, nor had the tribes traditionally accepted without question the right of a Sana-based government to rule them.

Moreover, Communist-bloc countries had immediately recognized the republican government and obviously intended to identify themselves with the cause of revolutionary change in Yemen as they had done in Iraq, Syria, and Egypt. This was one more expression of the Soviet objective to seek and foster the polarization of the Middle East into traditional and radical camps, with the West labeled as the protector of reaction and the U.S.S.R. as the champion of change and supporter of progress. If this polarization could be accomplished, the United States would be tied to a social and political order with a tenuous future, cut off from many of the most vigorous, if most troublesome, forces in Arab life. American interests required both the curtailment of Soviet influence wherever possible and identification with the cause of progress, development, and modernization.

Recognition was also related to the character and objectives of the new government. Whatever else may have been involved in al Sallal's coup d'état, it was an attempt to bring a more forward-looking regime to one of the most notoriously medieval Arab lands. As has already been noted, the 1962 movement did not take place in a vacuum, but had been preceded by other attempts to change rulers. It was undergirded by growing discontent of the small elite at home and Yemenis abroad with the reactionary outlook of the Imam's government. Little can be said in favor of the imamate under Ahmad, whose death provided the occasion of the revolt. He had contributed little to the progress of his country and had alienated many tribal rulers by executing members of their families. Some argue that his son, al Badr, was prepared to usher in a new day, but there was little either in his training for the throne or his inherent character to justify this view. The al Sallal revolt was genuine; it sprang from indigenous forces; its object was to bring a more modern era to the country. The United States could not quarrel with this objective.

Recognition was also important in relation to the new diplomacy of the Kennedy administration, which involved dialogue and persuasion. But how can dialogue be held with a government that is not recognized, or how can persuasion be applied without contact? The royalist group, then weak and in disarray, could be reached through the government of Saudi Arabia which was supporting it. Similarly the United States might have attempted to deal with the republicans through the intermediary of the U.A.R., but this would have been to denude the regime of any character of its own and to accept it merely as an Egyptian stooge. Also, it soon became apparent that British recognition would be long delayed, if given at all, for the revolutionary movement in Yemen would affect British interests in Aden. American recognition would make it possible for the United States to care for British interests in Yemen and possibly to moderate the impact of republican enthusiasm on the already perturbed situation in Aden colony.

Moved by these considerations, the United States kept the matter of recognition under constant review during the opening weeks of the Yemen struggle. The formal criteria for American recognition of any new government are three: that government must control a major part of the country, must not be preparing an attack on its neighbors, and must undertake the international obligations of the preceding regime.

By December, the United States decided that the republic had reasonable control over a significant portion of Yemeni territory. Royalist opposition was based on Saudi soil and had not rallied a majority of the tribes to its support. Republican control of the desert highlands was not complete, but neither had been the

Imam's when the throne still stood in Sana. There was a reasonable basis for recognition in the position of the republicans as controlling a major part of the country, with the political heartland of the cities firmly in their grasp.

The United States maintained close consultation with its allies, among whom recognition of the new regime had begun, and sought to determine whether the republicans were prepared to reaffirm the international obligations of the Imam's government and undertake to live at peace with Yemen's neighbors, this with special reference to border raids in the south. These undertakings were publicly announced in Sana, with a statement from Cairo welcoming the announcement. On the basis of these developments the United States extended its recognition to the Republic of Yemen on December 19, 1962. The timing was deliberate so that American recognition would appear to be neither unduly hasty nor unduly delayed, in line with the policy that had been adopted in recognizing Syria after it broke away from the U.A.R.

The Attempt to Secure Disengagement

After recognizing the republican regime, American diplomacy now turned to its central objectives of confining the struggle to Yemeni soil and preventing it from threatening the regimes in Saudi Arabia and Jordan. The main targets of this diplomacy lay in Amman, Cairo, and Riadh rather than in Sana, for it was the policies of Jordan, the U.A.R., and Saudi Arabia rather than of the republican regime in Yemen which generated the danger. Were it possible to persuade all three protagonists to withdraw from supporting the opposing sides of the struggle, leaving the affair to the Yemenis, the danger would be averted. But could this be done? To obtain the withdrawal of Jordan was not so difficult, since its resources obviously were unable to support continued and significant intervention; the perennially delicate political balance on which royal rule rested limited the king's ability to push a policy lacking full popular support, and the absence of threat to the territory of Jordan made the whole affair somewhat remote. Although it must have seemed a wearisome path of argument and pressure for the American Ambassador in Amman to traverse, Jordan was persuaded to withdraw its support.

Matters were different in Riadh, where there were ample resources of wealth to provide major and extended backing for the royalists. In taking refuge on Saudi soil, the royal family of Yemen had invoked the immemorial Arab tradition of hospitality and the defense of a guest who throws himself on his host's generosity. King Saud's position was sufficiently vulnerable that he could not but view with deep alarm the overthrow of a neighboring monarchy. In all this, the bad blood between Nasser and the Saudi royal house had generated deep and personal antipathy between the rulers in Cairo and the Saudi capital. For the Saudi king, it became both a matter of self-preservation and of *sharaf*—that particular brand of honor which rates so highly among Arabs. In addition, the degree of republican success in the early months of the revolution and the equivocal attitude of many of the tribal leaders made it clear that the royalist cause probably would be lost quickly without Saudi support. The republicans might not win a clear-cut victory, but the imamate as a regime and institution might well be doomed.

Cairo also felt that its *sharaf* was at stake in Yemen. President Nasser did not face any significant domestic opposition to his intervention, but he had committed the credibility of Egyptian commitments in responding to al Sallal's appeal for help. He had also placed revolutionary Egypt shoulder to shoulder with revolutionary Yemen in what he saw as the struggle to secure progress and modernity, this being in line with his recently announced policy of "unity of goals," which was to regulate Egypt's relations with other Arab states. As in the case of Saudi Arabia and the royalists, the U.A.R. questioned whether the republicans could maintain their position without Egyptian help. To abandon them before they were firmly entrenched would be to doom the revolutionary cause. Moreover, British hostility to the new Yemeni regime (centered in the Colonial Office and the governor of Aden Colony) aroused Egyptian feelings and fears. Sheikhs in British territory along the southeastern borders of Yemen gave at least spasmodic support to anti-republican tribesmen, with the active help or passive concurrence of the British authorities. These moves injected an element of "British colonialism" into the situation as the Egyptians saw it, to which their response was emotional and sharp.

Thus the task of persuading the Saudis and Egyptians to disengage was formidable. The Egyptians argued that the size of American oil holdings in Arabia made it possible for the United States to force the Saudis to cease and desist—if this was really what the Americans wanted. It was similarly argued by the Saudis that the size and character of American aid to Egypt made it possible for American pressure to force Nasser's withdrawal from the Yemen on the threat that aid (principally food) would be cut off. Both arguments were unrealistic. American oil holdings are private, not public, and the United States government in any case would not use its vital petroleum interest as a pawn in an intra-Arab dispute unless the danger to its own interests was very clear and very present. Equally, the United States would not face the loss of its position in the Arab world's most influential country for anything less than a major peril to its interests. Nor was it predictable that the threat of cutting off American surplus food would force the Egyptians out of Yemen. To judge by the post-Suez experience, the withdrawal of aid would only intensify Egypt's determination to stay and make it appeal to the Arab world and the Soviet bloc to witness how the American aid program was nothing more than a bludgeon for protecting traditional regimes and neocolonial positions.

Despite these difficulties the Kennedy administration pressed forward to seek some form of disengagement. The American ambassadors in Cairo and Jiddah were closely and continuously in dialogue with the U.A.R. and Saudi governments, which both showed an unusual degree of hospitality to discussion. Rarely in recent years has there been as intimate, frank, and sustained exchange of views and information as then took place. An ambassador cannot see a chief of state almost weekly for a continuing conversation on the same problem without breaking through the façades and formalities which often surround diplomatic contacts.

In Cairo the ambassador's task was to make clear the nature and sensitivity of American interests as they were affected by the Yemen dispute and to persuade President Nasser that it was in his interest, both in relation to the welfare of Egypt and to continued good relations with the United States, to cooperate in finding some way out of the impasse. In Jiddah the ambassador had similar concerns, with the additional responsibility of assuring King Saud that the United States stood behind the territorial integrity of his kingdom and the position of the royal regime, although this could not be expressed by becoming a partisan to Saudi intervention on behalf of the Imam. In addition to private assurances from the ambassador on behalf of his government, a small United States Air Force squadron was stationed in Saudi Arabia "for training purposes" as an earnest of intent to the Saudis and a warning to the U.A.R. that the United States was seriously concerned for the integrity of the Arab kingdom. Both ambassadors sought to secure a decrease of foreign intervention— from the Saudis by a reduction in supplies, facilities, and money given to the royalists; from the U.A.R. by limiting military action and reducing Egyptian troop strength in the country.

By March 1963, five months after revolution had broken out, the time seemed opportune to attempt a direct negotiation aimed at disengagement. For both intervening states, the prospects of a quick and easy victory were fading and the burdens of involvement were growing. Riadh seems to have underestimated the republican sentiment in Yemen, and to have concluded too easily that tribal warfare would rapidly make the Egyptian-republican, city-based position intolerable. On its part, Cairo had little comprehension of tribal ways or of the difficulties of fighting conclusive battles against desert guerrillas. It was baffled by the political inexperience and ineptness of the "brother revolutionaries" in the republican regime and by the lack of any fiscal or administrative machinery on which to build a new government. Tribal loyalties are notoriously fleeting; the longer fighting went on and the more inconclusive it became, the more willing the tribes were to take help from both sides but to commit themselves to neither. Moreover, what had started as Egyptian technical support for republican forces quickly became an Egyptian expeditionary army, bearing the brunt and bruises of battle. Casualties began to be reported in Cairo and disfigured corpses shipped home for burial. The U.A.R. was at a critical point where it either had to expand its participation, assuming growing military and political burdens, or seek some way out.

In these circumstances the United States took the initiative in seeking to obtain disengagement. Early in January 1963 it suggested that the United Nations Secretary-General send a special envoy to discuss the situation with the parties involved and attempt to work out with them some formula for disengagement. Ralph Bunche was charged with this responsibility and went to the area in March on a fact-finding mission. To emphasize American interest in disengagement and to re-enforce Dr. Bunche's efforts, President Kennedy sent Ellsworth Bunker to the Middle East as a special presidential emissary. With sustained patience and consummate skill, Ambassador Bunker worked with Cairo and Riadh until he was able to secure from the United Arab Republic and Saudi Arabia an agreement for mutual withdrawal, and the proposal was delivered to Secretary-General U Thant on April 13, 1963. Its chief provisions were cessation of Saudi help to the royalists, curtailment of the activities of the Imam and his family, and the expeditious withdrawal of Egyptian troops.

Although the withdrawal agreement seemed to set the stage for ending outside intervention, it was weaker than it appeared. Neither side trusted the other, for each was convinced that its opponent would use the other's withdrawal to strengthen his own position—not an unjustified suspicion. The agreement had come into being under American pressure and did not represent a change of heart in either party. While American pressure was effective to a point, it did not involve taking punitive action to enforce the agreement, and this was well understood. More important, as the machinery for observation did not exist, effective disengagement could not begin until an observer corps had been created and placed in position.

Could this have been done at once, it is possible, even probable, that disengagement would have commenced. Both parties stated their desire to begin withdrawal within one or two weeks. Having with some reluctance bowed to American pressure, they were in a mood to carry through the undertaking. But disengagement could not begin at once. It was suggested, and appeared to be acceptable to both parties, that a team of American observers could be formed quickly from the various military missions in Turkey, Iran, and Wheelus Base in Libya. Such a team could have taken position within a few days and would have provided the conditions for continued American pressure to fulfill the withdrawal commitment. But the United States was not prepared to undertake this responsibility. Instead it turned to Secretary-General U Thant and sought the creation of a United Nations observer force. In the American view, this could have been done by the Secretary-General on his own initiative, but U Thant felt he could not act without discussing the matter with members of the Security Council, a laborious and time-consuming process. By the time it was finished and U.N. observers began to arrive in Yemen, nearly three months had passed since the agreement had been signed.

During this period both the U.A.R. and Saudi Arabia continued and in some cases increased aid to their clients, so that they would be in a strong position to continue the struggle on their own. Supplies were stockpiled in Saudi territory, and arms continued to flow to the royalists. Egyptian troop strength increased and forays were made into border areas through which Saudi supplies were flowing. When the observation team arrived in July, both sides were more deeply entrenched than ever, and the mood of disengagement had weakened. Of course, each protagonist accused the other of taking the initiative in continued support to which "we must react." In fact, neither Saudi Arabia nor the U.A.R. was the sole villain in the piece, for both capitalized on the waiting period to sustain their intervention.

The subsequent history of the U.A.R.-Saudi Arabia confrontation in Yemen after the summer of 1964, is beyond the main interest of this chapter. With the failure of American efforts to secure disengagement, the situation came to rest in the hands of the intervening parties. The Arab League failed to play a mediating role, and the offer of some Arab states to act as intermediaries was not accepted. In the wake of the meeting of Arab chiefs of state in January 1964, the U.A.R. restored its diplomatic relations with Saudi Arabia and Jordan. The abdication of King Saud and the accession of his brother, Feisal, brought to the Arabian throne an astute and popular ruler, strengthening the position of Saudi Arabia both internally and in the Arab world. Most Arab countries seemed content to let President Nasser wrestle with his own difficulties in Yemen and watched King Feisal's increasingly effective opposition to the U.A.R. with quiet approbation. In August 1965, King Feisal and President Nasser negotiated a new withdrawal agreement, no more successful than the American attempt. At Khartoum in 1967, after the war with Israel, Nasser renewed his agreement with Feisal: U.A.R. troops were finally to withdraw and Saudi aid was to stop. This was at least a promise of disengagement, though no end of Yemen's civil war was in sight.

An Assessment

Since the American-sponsored disengagement agreement did not actually bring disengagement at the time, was American policy a failure? Those who answer "Yes"—and they are many—base their contention on the fact that the Yemeni conflict was not resolved. But this was not the most basic object of American policy in the situation. What the United States set out to do was not to secure Egyptian and Saudi withdrawal as an end in itself, but to insure the integrity and stability of Saudi Arabia and cushion that country against the shock of revolution in a neighboring state. Disengagement was sought as a means to that end. The means did not operate as fully as intended, but the end was nevertheless gained. With the accession of Feisal (hastened by the impact of the Yemeni struggle on Saudi Arabia), the government of that country was strengthened and today is reasonably stable and vigorous. The disengagement agreement gave the American ambassadors in Jiddah and Cairo a tool for pressure, warning, and continued representation which helped to keep the confrontation under control until relations between Cairo and Riadh could be restored. In particular, strenuous efforts were made to restrain the U.A.R. from bombing within the Saudi borders. Although disengagement was not brought about, the objective of American policy was achieved since the revolt in Yemen was prevented from involving either the stability of Saudi Arabia or a direct U.A.R.-Saudi military clash, and the oil resources of the Persian Gulf area were not jeopardized. The history of the affair was an illustration of how the course of day-by-day diplomacy may unwittingly obscure the basic objective of the foreign policy it seeks to serve.

The American approach to the problem of Yemen revived the issue whether the United States should play a police role in the Arab world, or be content to make its chief concern the protection of basic interests. When the disengagement agreement began to erode in the autumn and winter of 1963–64, there were those within the policy-making circles of the administration who pressed for a harder American line. Just what that line might be was not entirely clear—possibly stationing more aircraft in Saudi Arabia, patrolling the Yemeni-Saudi border by American planes which would shoot down any Yemeni or U.A.R. planes which crossed it, or cutting off all economic assistance to the U.A.R. Other policy-makers took a different view, advocating what may be called the "stew-in-your-own-juice" policy. Their argument was that danger to American interests had been contained and that the United States should not undertake to bail the U.A.R. out of its self-created difficulties.

Disengagement under American threat or pressure would enable President Nasser to say: "Imperialism is not dead. It forced me against my will to withdraw from the support of progress and the wishes of the people of Yemen. It was not that our intervention was unsuccessful, but that the Americans were too strong for us." If withdrawal were finally to come about as a result of domestic pressure and discontent within Egypt and the opposition of Saudi Arabia, it could be a sobering lesson to the U.A.R. when next it was tempted hastily to intervene in the affairs of another country. As the situation later developed, the U.A.R. has lost much reputation in the Arab world and has faced growing difficulties in its own domestic economy. This is a more effective lesson than one enforced by American strength. So long as the United States has and exercises its capability to defend its basic interests, it can afford to let Arab countries wrestle with, and learn the lessons of, their own problems.

Although the policy of a harder American line toward U.A.R. involvement in Yemen was rejected, the alternative of leaving the U.A.R. and Saudi Arabia to face their own difficulties was not as clearly and consciously adopted. After 1964 other factors began to operate, which altered American concern for the situation. The Johnson administration did not display as much patience toward Arab affairs as President Kennedy had, and President Johnson's identification, in Arab eyes, with a pro-Israel position made it difficult to continue the same openness of dialogue in Cairo that had emerged during the negotiations on Yemen. Meanwhile, the growing strength and stability of Saudi Arabia under King Feisal and his adroit diplomacy in dealing with the U.A.R. reduced American fears that further commitments would be needed to shore up the Saudi position. Disengagement negotiations between President Nasser and King Feisal, though inconclusive, seemed to offer more promise than any fresh attempt to impose an American solution. The growing demands of Viet Nam absorbed American attention and created a mood of impatience in the White House and State Department with the lesser and nagging problems of other areas. The administration appears to have felt that an extended effort had been made to be helpful to the U.A.R., but that the response was not such as to justify further strenuous efforts toward solving President Nasser's difficulties in Yemen. American interests appeared to be safe, and the best course appeared to be to leave the Yemen affair to those who had created it. Thus, in fact, a "stew-in-your-own-juice" policy was followed, until in time new events brought the goal of U.A.R. withdrawal unexpectedly to the point of realization.

This is to say that throughout the Yemen affair the guidelines of nonpolitical aid, nonalignment in Arab quarrels, and direct action to protect American interests operated to form the general approach of American policy. It is difficult to see what alternatives could have been followed. To abandon the U.A.R. to sole dependence for aid on the Communist bloc would not only have had serious repercussions on that country's position, but might have forced a closer Soviet-Egyptian cooperation in the Yemen, with the Soviets emerging as the chief supporters of the republican cause. As it is, it appears that the U.S.S.R. quietly cautioned President Nasser in 1965–66 that it would not support him in any drastic move in the Yemen which would result in a significant increase of American support for Saudi Arabia. Becoming a committed partisan of the Saudis—or the Egyptians for that matter—in the Yemen dispute would have polarized further the American position in the Arab world and tied the United States to a partner with an unpredictable future, harrowing the limits of American diplomatic maneuverability.

It does not appear that the United States could have intervened decisively without committing considerable resources to the task —an undertaking it was not prepared to assume since there was no major threat to American interests. American direct action was useful but could not go beyond diplomatic pressure and posting a few aircraft in Saudi Arabia unless the United States was prepared to risk military involvement. In short, the guidelines played their role not only because they represented the general approach of the United States to the Arab world, but also because they were inherent in the nature of the situation and the limits of American capability as related to American interests.

If the guidelines were present in the Yemen policy, so were many of the dilemmas they involved. Nonpartisanship in Arab disputes left the United States accepting the republican-royalist, U.A.R.-Saudi impasse as part of the *status quo*. It is significant that, aside from Saudi Arabia and the U.A.R., Arab states were not forward in blaming the United States for playing an indecisive role. At the time the disengagement was being undertaken, much of the Beirut press welcomed the possibility of a *pax Americana* in the Arab world. This welcome not only expressed a particularly Lebanese viewpoint, but was probably warmer in the prospect of a *pax* than its accomplishment, when the United States would have to move decisively to enforce its role.

The Sequel: Aden and South Arabia

If the impasse in Yemen had settled down to a static stalemate—as did the situation in Cyprus—it would not have continued particularly to concern the United States. The trouble was that after 1964 the U.A.R. position in Yemen began to exacerbate the problems of the neighboring Federation of South Arabia. Formed under British auspices from the Aden colony and some eighteen backcountry sheikhdoms under British protection, the Federation was to achieve independent status in 1968 as a member of the British Commonwealth.

As independence approached, the Federation was increasingly troubled by internal strife. Tensions between the tribal leaders and Aden nationalists, disagreement between those who wanted to follow a revolutionary path of change as exemplified in the U.A.R. and those who sought evolutionary development within the British Commonwealth, led to repeated violence and terrorism. Complicating the situation were the claims of Yemen to the territory, which both the Imam's government and the Yemen Republic called "occupied South Yemen." Some 75,000 Yemeni workers in the Aden colony formed a group which could be stirred up in support of this claim.

Since 1964 the U.A.R. had been increasingly active in fomenting and sustaining trouble in Aden. It assisted in training terrorists, supplied funds, supported extremist nationalist organizations and may have been involved directly in bombing incidents. The U.A.R. interest in Aden was not only an expression of Egypt's inherent revolutionary character and President Nasser's foreign activism, but was particularly related to the Egyptian dilemma in Yemen. As early as the winter of 1964, President Nasser had announced that Egyptian troops would not withdraw from Yemen while the British kept their position in Aden. Apparently he hoped to defend the continued Egyptian occupation as a safeguard against "British imperialism," deflecting attention from its role as a force fighting fellow-Arabs. When the Saudi-U.A.R. disengagement negotiations broke down and Egypt found itself faced in Yemen with a growing resistance from some factions of the republican government in addition to the royalists, a spill-over into Aden could well prove an irresistible temptation.

This possibility generated much concern. Egyptian action in Aden would not only increase instability in the area, but could, many argue, lead to a Soviet presence at the naval base in Aden after British withdrawal. Some thought that this would be the prelude to a Soviet-supported drive for control of the oil resources at the head of the Persian Gulf. In hindsight, it could be argued that by failing to get the U.A.R. out of Yemen and accepting the stalemate there, the United States had paved the way for a new and ominous Egyptian adventure.

In considering this argument, two questions must be asked. "Given the instruments available, could the United States have forced Nasser to withdraw from Yemen?" To this the writer's answer is "No." Short of some form of military action, possibly a threatening build-up of Saudi and American force inside Saudi Arabia, the U.A.R. could not have been forced to withdraw from Yemen and abandon its republican client there. The second question is: "Does the U.A.R. have the resources and is it in a condition to undertake another Yemen?"—which is what a major move into Aden would entail. This question can also be answered "No," especially in the aftermath of Egypt's disastrous defeat by Israel in 1967, which shattered its military capacity, heightened the country's economic weakness and distress and severely injured Nasser's already waning reputation among his Arab neighbors. A new foreign adventure, involving a conflict with fellow Arab states, would seem the last thing any responsible government would undertake while facing the tasks of rebuilding a nation after an overwhelming defeat. Yet the rational "No" is not necessarily the final answer, since the frustration of defeat and the desire to bolster waning national prestige could result in a decision to reassert Egyptian dominance by attempting another move in the Arab world. Much would depend on the attitude of the U.S.S.R. If it should again underwrite the U.A.R.'s military establishment and support an excursion into Aden as a useful ploy against the West (as it did in the Arab-Israel 1967 war), Egypt might well be tempted or pushed into an intervention in South Arabian affairs. But left to itself, the U.A.R. could no more seize Aden than it could seize Yemen. It had the capacity to make trouble, but not the capacity permanently to enlarge its political control of Arab affairs.

It was an ironic fact that at the very time the British were taking their departure from Aden, the Egyptian forces were not marching south in triumph but sailing back up the Red Sea to their homeland. The Yemen Republic had a new regime, replacing that of al Sallal. And the victorious new nationalists celebrating the independence of South Arabia at the end of November 1967 were the men of the National Liberation Front, a group which won its way to power by defeating not only the British-sponsored, conservative "federalists," but also the rival nationalist group nurtured and supported by Abdel Nasser.

Chapter VIII

Recurring Encounters

Running through the American approach to the Arab world has been a series of recurring encounters with attendant problems and strains, which have stood at the center of American-Arab relationship and account for many of the frustrations of American policy. The tactical guidelines in reference to which policies have been developed in recent years grew out of and were designed to deal with these encounters, but have been unable permanently to resolve them. They have lived on, circumscribing and interrupting the efforts of the United States to build and maintain a steady, effective posture in the Arab world. The domestic criticism of the ineffectiveness of American policy toward the Middle East has been due in large measure to failure to grasp the realities of these encounters and the limited ability of the United States to end them. Like creation as pictured by the Psalmist, the task has been to build an approach which of necessity must be "founded upon the seas and established upon the floods"—and the secret of this has not yet been discovered.

These recurring encounters are the Soviet-American rivalry, the Arab-Israel dispute, and the American-Arab tension. At worst they have resulted in direct confrontations, sometimes in conflict; at best they have been powerful subsurface currents carrying American policy in their grip whatever the pressure of immediate situations and interests. While each encounter has its own character and causes, all are so interrelated that a rise of temperature in one may rapidly heat up the others.

This was most recently shown by the situation resulting from the Arab-Israel crisis in the spring of 1967. What began as one more tragic clash between Israel and her Arab neighbors quickly involved the United States in a serious contention with the Soviet Union, and an even more serious confrontation with the Arab world. The conflict itself was the occasion of these, but not their sole cause, since there were elements in the Soviet-American and American-Arab tensions which went beyond the question of Israel. What the outbreak of hostilities did was to bring existing tensions to a new focus, add fresh elements of clashing interests to them, and fracture the fragile *modus vivendi* by which they had been held in uneasy check. The result may well be to write a new chapter in American policy toward the Middle East; certainly the American position was wrenched loose from its moorings to move with a turbulent current toward a future whose shoals and rapids are unknown.

Soviet-American Rivalry

Soviet-American rivalry in the Middle East derives from the fact that the region has major importance to both countries, which have pursued different, and often opposed, objectives in it. The nature of American interests requires stability, tranquility and orderly progress; Soviet interests have thrived on instability, tension and radical change. Behind these conflicting objectives lies the different role of the Middle East in relation to the two countries. For the United States the area is important in its own right as a communications center, related to Western responsibilities for global security, as the supplier of oil to a large segment of the non-Communist world, and as a strategic position for the containment of possible Soviet expansion. To the U.S.S.R. the Middle East has an importance in some ways different, in some ways similar. Soviet defense does not demand the use of Middle East communications, and the Soviet Union is itself an oil exporter not dependent on external petroleum supplies. Yet possession of Middle East oil and communication routes would give the Soviet Union an instrument of pressure which could be used to weaken the Western alliance and erode the cohesion of its members, especially in conjunction with other forces making inroads into Western unity. Moreover, the Soviet Union sees a threat to its security in the presence of Western bases and military strength in the area. Establishment of a dominant Russian position there would dissolve that threat, open an easier path to the developing nations of Africa, and form a base for turning the eastern flank of NATO.

In recent years the Soviet Union has developed other interests. One is the value of the Middle East as offering what may be a last chance to demonstrate the expansive powers of the Communist system under Russian leadership. Cuba proved a burdensome investment, efforts in Africa failed to build a significant Russian position, and in Southeast Asia it has been Chinese rather than Russian-led communism which played the major role. With the Sino-Soviet split and the challenge of China to Soviet leadership, it became ever more important for the Soviet Union to demonstrate the effectiveness and validity of its approach to the developing world. The Middle East—especially the Arab world—offered an attractive opportunity. Its relations with the West were eroding, the growing instability of its political life weakened its resistance to foreign penetration, and the Chinese had not built a position of power for themselves. Here, close to the borders of Russia, in an area of high strategic value to the West, was a region where Soviet success could pay handsome political and prestige dividends. Moreover, the Arab world was shot through with political and social discontent and was developing an indigenous, radical-revolutionary movement which might be molded toward Communist systems in the future. While the record of Soviet dealing with the Arab states makes it clear that the extension of communism per se has not had a first or most immediate priority, it remains a long-range goal toward which Soviet policy is dedicated to move.

In a sense, the basic problem of the United States and the Soviet Union was the same: as newcomers, to establish a permanent, effective, accepted place in the Arab world by which events could be shaped toward the desired objectives. Initially the United States had assets which gave it the edge over the U.S.S.R. Its existing relations to Arab petroleum resources had already created a community of interests with the Arab world. The postwar economic developments and modernization of the Middle East required Western resources and connections, and the United States was looked to as a supplier of these. The "American way" of technical achievement was widely admired and desired, while many of the leadership elite were at home with Western culture, technology and the English language.

With these assets the United States quickly built a commanding position, but it was a position under constant threat, the elements of which have been discussed in earlier chapters. Increasingly the American problem has been not to get into the Arab world, but to stay in, faced with problems of inter-Arab quarrels, political instability, the legacy of Western rule and the Arab fear of "neocolonialism," the new radical nationalism, the conservative-revolutionary split among the Arab states, and the changing position of the United States itself in capability and commitments in world affairs.

These elements affected and complicated the American position. Changing world political conditions and advances in technology had decreased the need for bases on Middle Eastern soil and had reduced the possibility of attack from without. Within the Arab world the threat came increasingly from intra-area strife and the arms race, as the Yemen affair and the Arab-Israel conflicts of 1956 and 1967 so clearly showed. At the same time the American position in relation to its allies having interests in the Middle East altered, as did their attitudes toward the role of the United States and its policy. France returned to the Arab world with a new policy reflecting De Gaulle's concept of an independent French role in international affairs; the Federal Republic of Germany developed its own ties with Arab countries; Italy and Japan became active in some parts of the region. The dominant position of the United States declined, and American policies on Arab problems became less definitive for members of the Western alliance than they had been in the past. By 1967 the United States could not count upon the general support of its allies for many of its Arab policies.

American policies and capabilities in the field of economic assistance in the Arab world also changed. The demands of Viet Nam and the domestic war on poverty and the perennial skepticism toward aid in Congress combined to reduce programs in size and to impose more political conditions. The important Food for Peace Program entered a new and diminished stage. In theory the United States could have substituted other forms of aid for food sales, but this would have required substantial dollar appropriations which Congress was not prepared to make, especially for countries like the U.A.R. with whom there were continuous and annoying problems.

The effect of these changes was compounded by the commitments of the United States in other parts of the world. Since 1963 the war in Viet Nam demanded more and more of the country's resources and absorbed the major part of the administration's attention. Senior policy-makers were impatient with the problems of other areas; in 1966–67 it was increasingly difficult to get high-level attention for any but the most dramatic crises in Arab affairs, such as the Israeli raid on El Samu in November 1966.

These changes eroded the American position in the Arab world. From its peak at the time of Suez it spasmodically declined, especially after 1964. When the crisis in Arab affairs came with the Arab-Israel war of 1967, the United States found itself only half-heartedly supported by its allies, unable to control either Israel or the Arab states, and without major influence in the Arab world that could counter successfully the Soviet position at the time. Clearly the American half of the Soviet-United States equation was in trouble.

The Soviet problem of getting into the Arab world began with none of the assets available to America. Russia had no prior economic or commercial ties of significance, its dedication to "godless communism" repelled the religious temper of the Muslim, and its political and cultural institutions were not of the pattern familiar to Arab leadership. Yet the Soviet Union had › other assets. Lacking any direct political responsibilities in the Arab world (either of its own or on behalf of its allies), it had freedom of action to pursue any policy which might serve its purposes. The dramatic transformation of Russian society since the revolution enabled it to offer a new mode of rapid social change to the impatient temper of Arab modernizers, a process which had dealt with problems akin to conditions in the Arab world. The massive Soviet political and economic position in world affairs could be put forward as an alternative to continued reliance upon (and in some Arab eyes, domination by) the former colonial Western powers and their allies—chiefly the United States.

With these assets the Soviet Union entered the Arab world through the Egyptian-Soviet arms deal in 1955. That transaction may have been only a tactical response to a tempting opportunity, but its enthusiastic reception in the Arab world and the inability of the West to checkmate it made clear that here was an effective point of entry into Arab affairs. Arms supply became and continued a principal instrument of Soviet activity. It met an urgently felt need in some Arab countries (especially the larger, more radical and nonaligned ones), could be done without undue drain on the Soviet economy, brought the Russians into contact with the political base of power in important Arab states (the military establishment), broke the traditional Western monopoly in arms supply, and increased the potential for instability in the region.

At the same time and initially through this instrument, the Soviets began to build a position of identification with the radical forces of social and political change. First in the U.A.R., then in Syria, Iraq, and Algeria, the U.S.S.R. provided economic and technical assistance and diplomatic support for "the national struggle." The Russian position during the Suez crisis in 1956 was widely heralded by Arabs as the basic reason for the Israeli-Anglo-French failure, even in those countries which feared the Soviets' objectives. By eschewing direct Communist activity, either through the support of local Communist movements or propaganda by its teams of technicians, the Soviets sought to picture themselves as a new anti-imperial, socially progressive, humanitarian-motivated, international force dedicated to furthering the aspirations of Arab nationalism.

The effect of this strategy was to build a position of growing, although circumscribed, influence in the U.A.R., with relations to Syria, Algeria and Iraq. Yet the Russians' initial expectation that their presence in the Arab world would immediately evoke a wide response—the goods in the new Soviet bazaar being so obviously more attractive than the stock of the discredited ex-colonialists that the Arabs would flock to the new merchants and leave the old bankrupt—was not fulfilled. Like the United States, the Soviets found themselves faced by periods of fluctuating influence and frustrating limitations. After their first dramatic success in Egypt and what appeared promising beginnings in Syria and Iraq, many of the factors working changes in the American position operated to curtail their efforts. The solidarity of the Communist world loosened, domestic economic needs within the Soviet Union affected the aid program (except for arms), Soviet commitments in Cuba and other parts of the world competed with the Middle East. Russian economic and political support was welcomed in some Arab countries but did not generate a connection so overwhelming as to give the Soviets a large and readily invoked influence on Arab national policies. Above all, Arab nationalism proved unexpectedly resistant to attempts to control or channel it toward Communist objectives. Russia's clients were in dispute with each other and used their Russian-supplied weapons in unprofitable adventures such as the Egyptian excursion into Yemen.

In view of these limitations the U.S.S.R. seemed content to settle for a continuing presence in the Arab world, which with patience might gradually lead to a sphere of larger influence. But after 1964 the situation began to change. American influence in Egypt waned, partly as a result of the U.A.R.'s own actions, partly because of a lack of sophistication in American policy which made it unwilling to continue the important program of food sales to a government of which so many congressmen disapproved. This made President Nasser more dependent on the Soviet Union and offered the Russians opportunities for a more dominant role than had been possible in the past. At the same time the stalemate in Yemen, continuing strain between Syria and the U.A.R., King Feisal's success in circumscribing President Nasser's influence, and the mounting economic difficulties of Arab socialism so threatened the U.A.R. that the Soviets had to face the possibility of either writing off their investment there or moving further to support it. The dramatic and unheralded removal of Khrushchev in 1964 brought a new fluidity to Arab-Soviet relations, cautioning the leaders of Russia's client states that they could not count upon the continuation of past Soviet policy but would have to come to terms with a new Soviet leadership. The Soviets moved to patch up Syrian-Egyptian relations and at the same time strengthened their efforts in Syria in the hope of developing an alternate base to the U.A.R. from which they had failed to get dividends as large as their investment seemed to warrant.

Yet attempts to increase the sphere of Soviet influence necessarily fell short of any policy which would set the U.S.S.R. on a collision course with the United States. After 1958 it was clear that neither Russia nor the United States would risk a Middle East policy which would be a direct challenge to the other; the nuclear stalemate was too complete, the consequences of global war too catastrophic to risk brinkmanship in the Arab world. The Soviet problem was to maintain and increase its presence, continue to circumscribe American influence, gain wider acceptance among the Arabs, and sharpen its image as the anti-imperialist friend and supporter of Arab causes by policies which avoided a military confrontation with America.

The new intensity in the Arab-Israel dispute which began to emerge in 1966 and 1967 gave the Soviets an attractive opportunity to pursue these objectives. The Soviet attitude toward Israel was based principally on the fact that Israel's presence could be counted upon as a perennial cause of problems and instability in the Arab world; this seems to be the reason the Soviet Union voted for the creation of Israel in the first place. With American attention and resources diverted to South-

east Asia, British difficulties in Aden, and the independent
policy of France, the risk of vigorous Western action was minimal.

The stunning Arab military defeat of June 1967 obviously
caught the Soviet Union off guard. Not only had the weapons
they supplied been captured or destroyed, but the inherent
weakness and inefficiency of their clients' military systems had
been starkly revealed. There is some evidence that the U.A.R.
committed itself far beyond Soviet desires; the removal of
United Nations observer forces from Sinai and the closing of
the Straits of Tiran were apparently done without consultation
with Moscow. It seems clear that the Soviets did not expect active
warfare and believed they could restrain the Egyptians from
aggressive action—hoping at the same time that the United
States could similarly restrain Israel.

When this expectation failed, with war and defeat coming
suddenly and without preparation, the Soviets took two lines
of action. They became the champions of the Arab cause at
the United Nations, clamoring for the condemnation of Israel
and the withdrawal of its forces from Arab territory and sum-
moning the General Assembly for an extended propaganda
attack on Israel and its supporters—chiefly the United States.
At the same time they moved swiftly to begin re-equipping the
shattered Egyptian army, proffered arms to Jordan, and cultivated high-level contacts with Algeria, Syria, and the U.A.R.
They also established a naval presence at the mouth of the
Suez Canal as a gesture of support to the U.A.R. and an
ostensible warning to Israel, which occupied the east bank of
the canal and claimed the right to patrol canal waters.

Obviously the Soviets suffered losses in this affair. For a
decade they had poured arms into Egypt and Syria only to see
them vanish in a maelstrom of lightning defeat. In the moment
of conflict they failed to give military support to their clients,
making it apparent to the Arab world that while they would
speak up on behalf of the Arab cause they would not fight for
it. At the United Nations, both in the Security Council and the
General Assembly, they were unable to force through their
resolution condemning Israel and calling for the withdrawal of

its troops from Arab soil. They proved unable to control their clients on the brink of conflict with Israel, and equally unable to win their acceptance for a compromise resolution at the General Assembly when the resolutions based on Arab desires had failed. It was evident that the U.S.S.R. was not as strong a friend as the Arabs had hoped, nor did it have as much control over them as might have served to avoid the last step toward conflict and bring about the first step toward peace.

In their future relations with the Arab world the Soviets faced renewed problems. Undoubtedly their clients would press them to write off the debt for lost military equipment; even were they willing to do this, would they be prepared to run the risk of seeing a new supply go down the drain of Arab inefficiency? And could they stop short at arms supply, refusing other types of aid urgently needed to rebuild shattered national economies? The U.S.S.R. had demonstrated its unwillingness to become the U.A.R.'s supermarket when American food aid ended in 1966. In the desperation to which Egypt was reduced by defeat—the Suez Canal closed, important oil resources in Israeli hands, tourism halted, Western loans unavailable, the cotton crop serevely damaged by disease—could it continue this policy and retain significant influence in future Egyptian developments? Yet the pressing domestic demands of the Russian economy would mean that it would take some sacrifice to supply food and capital goods, and this would be justified only if the resulting dividends were substantial.

These difficulties were a part of the general limits on Soviet diplomacy in the Middle East. It had not been able directly to challenge the United States nor to rally the support of the world community in the United Nations. While publicly and loudly supporting the Arab cause it was at the same time privately urging the Arabs to come to some accommodation with Israel. Clearly, instability in the Arab world had come to such a point that even the Soviets found it in their interest to temper reckless policies. Arab representatives were angered; Algeria and Syria in particular showed sharp resistance to Soviet efforts seeking a *modus vivendi* between the Arab states and Israel. At the time of the Cuba crisis, one Arab chief of state had observed: "This proves that the Soviets will not go out on a limb for the sake of a small, third country. They did not defend Cuba, and they will not defend us." If this lesson had been forgotten, 1967 taught it afresh to the Arabs.

Yet these liabilities do not warrant the conclusion that the Soviets suffered a disastrous setback. On the contrary, they emerged from the crisis with a new identification with the Arab world and with fresh opportunities for influence. Too much has been made of the Soviet unwillingness to fight for the Arab cause; it is to be doubted whether many Arab leaders ever expected them to do so. The effect of a sustained and strident voice on behalf of the Arabs was powerful, and the Arabs were both moved and grateful that one of the world's great powers spoke up for them, especially in the councils of the United Nations and in opposition to the United States. Whatever the ultimate result, the Soviet action will long be remembered (as will the Soviet financing of the High Dam when the West rejected it) and will permanently enhance the Russian image in Arab eyes. Moreover, this support was given to the one cause which overarches all the disputes and tensions between the Arab states and was most calculated to fan the flames of anti-Western and anti-American feeling. At least for the time being, the Soviets broke out of their identification with the radical Arab camp to become the champion of all Arabs, even those in the conservative states which had been wary of any connection with Communist Russia.

The policy of re-equipping Arab armies after their defeat offered new possibilities of penetration and influence to the Soviets. Arms are not the priority need for shattered and defeated nations, but Arab leaders clamored for them as a protection against further Israeli action and a symbol that the Arab spirit was not cowed or broken. In re-supplying arms the Soviets could argue that the cause of defeat was not the equipment, but the lack of Arab ability to use it. "If you had only allowed us to train you better, you would not have been so easily defeated." In the past, Arab governments were wary of large military training missions, moved by national pride and fear of undue Soviet influence. Now training missions could be made a precondition for arms supply, carrying the Soviets into the heart of the military establishment which is the basis of political power in many Arab countries.

The catastrophic state of some Arab economies in the aftermath of war and the unlikelihood that the West would move to help them gave Soviet economic and technical assistance a new setting. It was true that Soviet resources in food, machinery and consumer goods are limited and that help in these fields would be likely to come in driblets rather than in a permanent and dependable stream. But in an hour of desperate need every drop counts, even though it must be purchased at a price the recipient dislikes but cannot afford to refuse. Unless counterbalanced by aid from other sources, the Egyptian economy might be driven into such dependence upon the Soviet Union and its allies that its freedom of action virtually would disappear.

In contrast to these advantages the United States emerged with a heavy burden of lost influence in the Arab world. The major Arab countries broke diplomatic relations with it and to judge by the time it took to mend Anglo-French relations after the 1956 crisis, they would be restored only slowly. Aid programs were halted and could be reinstituted with great difficulty and only over strong congressional and popular opposition (except possibly for Jordan and Saudi Arabia). The Arab identification of Israel as the chosen instrument of American policy had been greatly sharpened and would plague the future American position for many years to come. American private organizations in the Arab world (universities, foundations, educational exchanges, relief and philanthropic programs), which had been an important element in the American presence, were forced to suspend their work, remove their personnel, and, in some cases, surrender their property to sequestration. Oil shipments in American tankers ceased, and some of the important pipelines were closed down. While this stoppage might be temporary, it bespoke an Arab reaction to American policy much deeper and sharper than that which accompanied the 1948 and 1956 crises.

To be sure, the Arab world would continue to profit by a Western economic connection and share a mutuality of interests in oil production with the United States. In time these factors might operate to restore some of the American position, but they could not eradicate the intensified Arab conviction that the United States had made Israel its chief instrument and thus could never be a friend of the Arabs.

Diplomatically the United States position was a mixture of strength and weakness. On the credit side was its firm and successful stand in the Security Council for a realistic cease-fire —a position to which the Soviets finally acceded. In the General Assembly it avoided a wordy propaganda battle with the Soviets, helped to defeat the "nonaligned" resolution calling for Israel's unconditional withdrawal from occupied territories, and consistently supported moderate proposals designed to bring peace to the area, in particular the Latin American resolution. Yet, like the Soviet Union, it was unable to secure the adoption of a resolution based on its position. As debits must also be counted the failure of the United States to secure support from allies who refused to rally to the American plan for opening the Straits of Tiran and were unwilling to put forward suggested resolutions to the Security Council. Moreover, the United States hedged on one of its most reiterated policies in the Middle East, the territorial integrity of all existing states. In view of the special United States relations with Israel and the realities of Arab-Israel border disputes, this was probably unavoidable, yet it weakened the credibility of American undertakings and played directly into Soviet and Arab hands. Even the unanimous adoption by the Security Council in November 1967 of a resolution setting forth principles of a settlement did not satisfy the Arabs on this point, for it was the United States that would not specify Israel's withdrawal from *all* occupied territories.

Nor was the United States successful in demonstrating that it could restrain as well as support Israel. Up to the actual outbreak of hostilities, Washington was pressing Israel to refrain from overt action while further attempts were being made to work out some solution to the problem of the Gulf of Aqaba;

these efforts collapsed when Israel decided to attack. Nor were American representations opposing the Israeli annexation of Jordanian Jerusalem any more successful. It seemed clear that in the future Israel's policies would be even less responsive to American pressure than they had been in the past.

Thus, after twenty years (dating from the Truman Doctrine in 1947) the American-Soviet competition in the Middle East remained an unresolved challenge to the diplomacy of the United States. Despite American efforts, Russia had been able to penetrate the Arab world and establish a significant presence in its affairs. That presence was circumscribed by many factors —Arab nationalism, inter-Arab quarrels, American military strength, the limited resources of the Soviet Union for supplying nonmilitary aid. The Soviets neither controlled significant parts of the Middle East nor were they in a position overtly to challenge the Western position. But 1967 showed they had made deep inroads into American relations with the Arabs and could use their position in the Middle East as a warning and a counter to American-Communist confrontations elsewhere, as in Southeast Asia. In the aftermath of the Arab-Israel war the Soviets faced new problems of meeting Arab expectations and bearing the burden of unilateral assistance to some of their economies. These difficulties were complicated by an international situation where their inability to obtain world diplomatic support for their Arab policies had been plainly revealed. Yet they had been able to sharpen their identification with some of the leading Arab states, ride a riotous wave of anti-American feeling throughout the length and breadth of the Arab world, and display their ability to stir up the area against Western interests.

Whether or not the Soviet position would be stronger in the future than in the past probably depended more on their own actions than on countervailing American policy. If they continued to pursue objectives of fostering and arming Arab revolution, exacerbating inter-Arab quarrels and identifying themselves with the Arab cause against Israel, the United States would be hard pressed to counter them, especially in view of the liabilities with which it emerged from the 1967 experience. The American-Soviet encounter would continue to live on as one of the most basic and disturbing challenges to the American approach to the Arab world.

The Arab-Israel Dispute

Like the Soviet-American encounter, the Arab-Israel dispute has dogged the path of American diplomacy in the Middle East since the end of the Second World War. It has been an intractable and complicating problem which continuously has burdened the American approach to the Arab world. Since the United States is not directly a party to the dispute, which lies between sovereign governments in the area, its options have been limited and its influence circumscribed.

The history of this tragic struggle is too familiar to require recapitulation. Many hoped that after two defeats at Israel's hands in 1948 and 1956, the Arabs would acquiesce in the fact of Israel's existence, turn their attention to the pressing problems of nation-building and gradually make their peace with the situation. Some evidence of such an accommodation could be found in the moderate policies of Jordan, Bourguiba's voice of reason from Tunisia, and the practical disinterest of Morocco, Libya and Saudi Arabia in activating the conflict. Only in revolutionary Syria and the U.A.R. and to a lesser extent in Algeria, did the Palestine question repeatedly take precedence over domestic affairs. The growing disunity between Arab states seemed to inhibit any effective collective action, or even any collective action at all. The radical and conservative camps in the Arab world were in sharp dispute, the Arab Unified Command was disintegrating, the Syrian and U.A.R. potential for leadership diminishing. It seemed as though patience, time and the growing pressures of national development might carry the Arab-Israel dispute to at least the threshold of accommodation.

Yet the events of 1966–67 showed that the heat of the dispute was as alive as ever in the Arab mind, once the ashes had been blown away. Arab actions in the spring of that year reflected more the spirit of 1948 than of 1956: a general reaction against the very existence of Israel rather than a limited response to a localized military action. Whatever their past attitudes had been, the Arabs now displayed an unexpected unanimity of response for which many observers were unprepared. It seemed as though the dispute had taken on the character of a "Hundred Years' War," with renewed conflict every decade.

The reasons for the unexpected outbreak of war in 1967 were varied. On the Arab side, one basic factor was the memory and continued impact of 1956, largely forgotten by the outside world. From the events of 1956 Arab leaders (especially President Nasser) drew three conclusions. The first was that Israel would "try it again" when the circumstances were favorable. The second was that never again could the Arabs risk having their armed forces unmobilized when there were indications of possible Israeli aggressive action. The third was that at the moment of crisis, the international community would move to stop a major conflict, as it did in 1956. This point was frequently made by Egyptian leaders as a reason why an all-out Arab war against Israel would not succeed. World forces stopped Israel, France and Great Britain in 1956, they argued, and would stop the Arabs in 1966.

After the Israeli raid on the Jordanian village of El Samu in November of 1966, Arab leaders apparently believed that Israel was moving toward an aggressive policy which might result in military action against Syria. Premier Eshkol hinted as much in one of his speeches to the Knesset in the spring of 1967. Shortly thereafter, significant amounts of heavy military equipment were not on display at Israel's independence day parade, as in previous years. Where were they? The Soviets apparently supplied an answer when they informed the Syrians that their intelligence had reported a build-up of Israeli forces on the Syrian border, although Eshkol's invitation to the Soviet Ambassador to see for himself met with a refusal. Syrian and Egyptian intelligence later claimed to have their own information confirming the Soviet report. Whether or not it was true, the important thing is that the Egyptian and Syrians were of a mind to believe it in view of Egypt's having been caught off guard in 1956. They then activated the second conclusion from the 1956 experience—that when Israeli action seemed in the making, the Arabs should forestall it by mobilizing their own military might; hence the rapid placement of the Egyptian army in Sinai and the aggressive statements of the Egyptian and Syrian governments. But all this was within the context of the third conclusion: that the world community could be depended upon to stop an Arab-Israel war. It seems to have been the assumption on which President Nasser based his hope that he could win a political victory without risking actual war.

To 1956 were added other factors. One was the relationship between Syria and the U.A.R. Syria had always claimed proprietary leadership in the Arab cause and followed a policy of border belligerency toward Israel, especially when the latter attempted to utilize the demilitarized zones along the border.

Under Soviet prodding for a rapprochement with Syria, and in line with his policy of seeking some measure of control over the armed forces of other Arab states (lest their actions against Israel involve Egypt in unplanned hostilities), President Nasser concluded a mutual defense pact with Damascus in September 1966. After the disastrous Israeli-Syrian air encounter in April 1967, the Syrians had been pressing the U.A.R. to activate its commitment. This situation led, when the temperature rose again in May, to the U.A.R.'s request for the recall of UNEF, so that its troops would face those of Israel directly at the border, and to the closing of the Gulf of Aqaba, which Israel had warned would be considered a *casus belli*. It is probable that initially President Nasser had not contemplated either of these actions, but was swept along by the current of events and tempted by the opportunity to wipe out the 1956 stain on the Egyptian escutcheon by regaining control of the Gulf of Aqaba. The proclamation of an international status for the Gulf was the only gain Israel had made by her action eleven years earlier and thus symbolized both her use of force and the Egyptian defeat at that time.

At the same time the U.A.R. was struggling to break out of its circle of declining influence in the Arab world. The Yemen war, the unsuccessful confrontation with Saudi Arabia, the difficulties of Arab socialism and the sharp disputes between Arab states had curtailed the position of the U.A.R. and President Nasser. The unexpectedly wide and enthusiastic acclaim given Egypt by the Arab world when it regained control of the Straits of Tiran seemed to promise a unanimity of support which had been lacking in 1956 and could restore the U.A.R. to a position of leadership. Given the conviction that international forces would prevent a major conflict, the temptation for a dramatic political victory was scarcely to be resisted.

The details of Soviet involvement in this series of events are difficult to determine. Their bonds with and investment in Syria and the U.A.R. were such that they could not completely turn their backs on their clients at a moment of crisis. On one hand, it seems clear that they did not expect active hostilities and thought they might control Egypt and Syria short of recourse to armed conflict. They also probably overestimated the power of the United States to control Israel. On the other hand, by fostering a major threat to the American position in the Arab world, they could make political gains and also serve notice that if the United States persisted in making difficulty for the Soviets in Southeast Asia, they could counter by raising a storm in the Middle East.

Underlying the immediate Arab causes of conflict are two continuing aspects of the Arab-Israel tension which, more than any others, kept the dispute alive. The first was the failure to achieve any solution to the Arab refugee problem. For all Arabs, the refugee is the symbol of the loss of Palestine and of the inherent "aggressive, anti-Arab" nature of Israel. Israel's failure to implement the repeated resolutions of the United Nations (to whose authority Israel owed its own existence), its refusal to accept any responsibility for the existence of the refugees and its lack of interest in contributing toward a solution continuously and deeply stirred Arab feelings for two decades. The festering sore the refugees represented had as its natural consequences movements like the Palestine Liberation Organization, leaders like Ahmed Shukairy, and renewed opportunities for aggressive Arab policies. With no solution to the refugee problem to which Israel contributed, and which was based on the right of Palestinians to return to their homes and property, it was inevitable that there should be another round of conflict and a continuing, bitter dedication to righting what the Arabs saw as an intolerable and inhuman wrong.

The second factor lay in the connection (in the Arab mind) between Israel and neocolonialism, imperialism and the designs of the Western world to divide and control the Arabs. The background for this has been given in Chapter III; it lay in the reaction of the emerging Arab states against their past domination by Western powers. Israel came to the Arab world as a foreign creation, brought into being by Western diplomatic and financial power in disregard of the wishes of the Arab inhabitants of Palestine. Its continued existence was only possible because it was generously supplied with arms, money and support by the Western powers, chiefly the United States. It was easy for the Arabs to conclude from this that Israel was a chosen instrument of British and American policy, designed to keep the Arab world tense and troubled, divided and ineffective. The connection so often made by Arab leaders between Zionism and imperialism is not fortuitous; it stems from the deep suspicion of Western motives and the belief that Israel was forced on the Arab world by the great powers and chiefly in their interest. To the Arab, Israel is more than Israel; it is the fact and symbol of the continuation of foreign interference in Arab destiny against which Arab nationalism has struggled since the First World War, and against which it will continue to struggle.

On its part, Israel was equally determined to continue and safeguard its existence. Since the summer of 1966 Syria had been mounting border raids and guerrilla attacks which the Israeli government found it increasingly impossible to meet with soft answers. Not only did the actual loss of life and threat to border settlements become unbearable, but domestic discontent on other issues (such as unemployment and rising prices) pressed upon the Eshkol government. The El Samu raid probably was due in part to the necessity for the government to display an aggressive response to the one problem which was never absent from the Israeli mind: the encircling, hostile Arab world. But this raid did not dampen the Syrian temper; on the contrary, raiding continued, culminating in an air battle in which the Syrians were defeated but unrepentant. In the face of such acts and the accompanying chorus of threats from Syria, it is not surprising that Premier Eshkol warned Syria that Israeli patience was reaching its limit, thus setting in motion the chain of events which led to conflict.

The events of 1956 were a backdrop to the Israeli attitude as well as to the Arab. Then Israel had been forced by international pressure to give up its gains, but subsequently the same international forces were unable to prevent the resumption of border attacks which had triggered the 1956 action. Despite vague assurances from the United States, the Suez Canal had not been opened to Israeli shipping. Israel concluded that U.N. action and international guarantees had not proved effective in increasing its security nor were they likely to meet the problems of the future. This was particularly relevant to the U.A.R. action in regaining control of the Gulf of Aqaba. Elath had become the principal port for Israel's petroleum supply, enabling it to have access to the East despite the barring of the Suez Canal. An Arab threat to this important economic and security interest could not be accepted with impunity. When immediate and strong action was not taken by international forces to reopen the Gulf, Israel concluded that it had no protection but in its own action; the slow process of international diplomacy and the ineffectiveness of international guarantees did not offer a dependable substitute.

Thus, as the Arab-Israel dispute moved toward possible armed conflict, there were strong forces which believed that only by Israel's strength and at its own initiative could it be made secure. Moshe Dayan, identified with this view, argued that the Arab states would never come to terms with Israel so long as it appeared to be simply an international ward whose future would be imperiled if foreign support were withdrawn. Israel had to demonstrate by its own action and with its own resources that it was able to defeat the Arabs, should they challenge Israel's vital interests. The inclusion of Dayan in the Eshkol government on June 2, together with the failure of other states to do anything to assure free passage through the Straits of Tiran, made it virtually certain that Israel would use force to assert its rights as it saw them.

Running through Israel's attitudes and policies have been two basic factors without which its courses of action cannot be understood. The first is the concept that Israel has a "right to exist." This phrase, so widely used during the 1967 crisis, is not simply the claim that an existing state, created by the United Nations and a member of that organization, cannot rightfully be delivered to the hostility of its neighbors by the world community. To many in the world Jewish community, it is the assertion that the selfhood of Judaic consciousness demands and deserves a corporate political and social organism. The feeling was heightened by the terrible decimation of European Jewry under Hitler. Because the original Jewish organism was created and flourished in Palestine, the Zionist movement claimed a right to a place in Palestine, transcending that of later inhabitants even though they may have lived in the country for as long as the original Jewish people had. This is the point of major conflict between Arab and Israeli. To the Arab, every overture for peace or plea for accommodation is per se a device to deprive him of his own heritage in Palestine in favor of a foreign, historically remote, culturally alien group.

Yet to Israel and to Zionists outside Israel this right is the very essence of its existence. To surrender that concept in favor of a "reservation" for Jews as a persecuted minority would be to deny the very genius of Jewish life and history as expressed in the concept of Zionism. Hence the insistence by some Jews that any opposition to Israel is a form of anti-Semitism, that is, a denial of an inherent right to the Jewish people (as they themselves define it). Hence also the pressure during the 1967 crisis on Western governments, churches, and leading personalities to affirm the "right of Israel to exist" since nothing short of this recognition would give Israel a charter of absolute legitimacy. Yet this claim goes far beyond what many non-Jews are prepared to support, despite their sympathy with victims of persecution, their sense of guilt for the treatment accorded the Jews in the West, and their unwillingness to allow the destruction of any existing society.

The second Israeli attitude is related to the first; if Israel is to express the genius of Jewish selfhood it must develop in its own way, untrammeled by controls from without. It cannot be the permanent ward of someone else; it must be free to develop its own political, religious and social life, and to pursue its own national policies. At times this idea has led to sharp differences between Israel and world Zionist organizations which claim some proprietary right in Israel's existence. It also has led, and increasingly may lead, to strains between Israel and the foreign states and communities which support it. Israel owes its original creation and initial security to the political and financial support of world powers, among which the United States played a leading role. Many in the West assumed that Israeli interests and foreign interests coincided to a reasonable degree and that Israeli policies would not run counter to the major interests of its backers. But the more Israel has developed its own unique character as a sovereign and independent state, the more it has necessarily pursued policies based upon its own interests as Israel itself sees them. In recent years these interests have not inevitably coincided with those of Israel's friends abroad. How to continue to obtain the measure of foreign support needed, yet retain freedom of action to pursue policies of its own making, is one of Israel's constant problems. It is one problem which starkly emerged from the 1967 crisis when it was not in the interest of the United States to have Israel take to arms as the final arbiter of Arab hostility, nor to have it continue to occupy Arab territory or annex the Jordanian portion of Jerusalem. These actions served Israel's ends, but not American interests, and created a situation which must affect the future of American-Israeli relations.

Encapsulated in the 1967 crisis are the problems which the Arab-Israel dispute created for American policy over the years. It has been the most recurrent threat to the stability of the Arab world—and stability is one of America's principal concerns. Three times in nineteen years conflicts between Israel and its Arab neighbors have shaken the area. After each conflict there was serious instability in some Arab states: the Egyptian revolution and the series of coups in Syria in the aftermath of 1948; the Iraq revolution; the creation (then breakup) of the Syrian-Egyptian union; and the Lebanese troubles after 1956. In the aftermath of 1967 it seemed probable that chaotic changes might once again occur. The existing regimes in Syria and the U.A.R. could not be predicted to remain in power once the full weight of defeat had been felt, and it seemed unlikely that the alternatives to them would be more stable or moderate governments. The position of King Hussein, even the continuance of Jordan as a state, were gravely imperiled. The very scope of the Arab world's involvement in the 1967 fighting and the extent of the defeat will probably increase rather than diminish the instability of the Arab regimes.

At the same time the Arab-Israel dispute continuously has fostered the image of the United States as a principal actor in neocolonial and Western designs on the Arab world. This has led to wild and unfounded accusations on the part of some Arab leaders, yet accusations from which the United States has not been able to escape and which complicate the tasks of its diplomacy. Some think that too much importance has been given to Arab attitudes which, they maintain, shift rapidly and give way before the pressure of national interests. But this has not been the case with the American connection with Israel and the conclusions the Arabs have drawn from it. While the object of a foreign policy can never be confined to "winning friends," "influencing people" is an essential instrument for successful diplomacy. The image of America as involved in the "aggressive" intents of "Western imperialism" and of Israel has been a serious barrier to building permanent and good relations with the Arabs.

Moreover, the Arab-Israel dispute has limited the freedom of the United States in formulating its policies toward the Arab world. America's past commitments to Israel and the pressure of Israel's supporters in the United States exercise a limiting power over American policy. This not only affects American actions toward Israel but must be taken into account when Arab questions are under consideration. It can be argued that it would be in the interest of the United States to assist in rebuilding the U.A.R.'s shattered economy, but it is predictable that for this and other reasons such a move would arouse a storm of angry protest which only the bravest congressman could contemplate defying. In seeking to rebuild its position in the Arab world, the United States will be pressed to center upon those conservative countries which did not take leadership in the 1967 crisis, and thus are not so deeply tagged with the label of anti-Israeli hostility as the revolutionary governments. Yet it may well be that the revolutionary states will affect the future destiny of the Arab world more than the conservative ones, and that American interests would best be served by seeking to rebuild a useful relation with them. The difficulty has been that in any policy toward the Arab world the United States has had to stop, look, and listen to how it might affect Israel and what the domestic response of Israel's supporters to it would be. This has not led to the uniform adoption of policies favoring Israel, but it is a constantly inhibiting factor in the freedom of choice which the United States has in dealing with the Arab world.

Like the Soviet-American encounter, the Arab-Israel dispute has been beyond the capacity of the United States to resolve. It has worked at the question through the United Nations, by supporting attempts to solve the refugee problem, and by putting pressure on the contending parties—with increasing ineffectiveness. It has attempted to keep its dealings with Israel and the Arab states in balance, supplying arms and aid to both. At times it has sought to put the dispute in the "ice box" in its dealings with Arab governments by a frank and mutual recognition of basic differences regarding the matter and an agreement not to let these intrude on mutually profitable relations. But the problem did not stay under refrigeration for long and it will continue to be a constant and perplexing dimension of the American approach to the Arab world.

The American-Arab Tension

The foregoing paragraphs would seem to imply that the American relation to Israel is the whole substance of the tension between the United States and the Arab world. Certainly it has been a continuous and important factor yet, as has been pointed out earlier, even if Israel had never come into existence, the United States would probably have had difficulties in its Arab relations.

The reasons for this conclusion have already been discussed in various contexts in this study. Basically they spring from the fact that the objectives of the United States in the Middle East are not shared by the Arab states and at times run counter to their own national interests. The objectives of containing Soviet expansion has clashed with the interest of some Arab governments in having a counterpoise to the American and Western position, and in securing military and economic aid from a non-Western source. The American interest in defense of the area with its accompanying pressure for Western-supported regional defense pacts and the use of military facilities grated on the nationalist spirit and independence of Arab states. Before and during the Dulles period, pressure for Arab alignment with the West stirred fears that the Arabs would once again be bound to the chariot wheel of Western imperialism and denied their own independent place in world affairs. In general, the priorities which the Arab world saw as essential for its own development in independence were at variance with the priorities of American policy.

To this was added the suspicions created by the rise of American power in and near the Middle East. Before the Second World War the American presence had been a threat to no one; it did not involve bases, arms, supplies, fleets, troops, or significant diplomatic pressure. But after the war, the United States rapidly became the most powerful and ubiquitous foreign presence in the area. It supported the military establishments of the northern tier, had bases in Morocco, Libya, Turkey and Saudi Arabia, and its powerful Sixth Fleet was always just beyond the horizon. What Great Britain once was the United States had now become in Arab eyes—the policeman of the world, with a capacity to intervene in Arab affairs. This made for recurrent suspicion of the United States and its policies; it was too powerful, too omnipresent, too much like the imperial powers of the past to be accepted with ease of mind.

Moreover, the United States had special interests in the Arab world which tended to identify it with the more conservative regimes of Saudi Arabia, Jordan, Morocco, and Libya. As the radical temper of the Arab world grew and some of the largest countries took the path of revolutionary change, the American relation to traditional states was interpreted as setting it in opposition to the revolutionary movement. This was taken both as evidence of American hostility to change and progress, and as a form of "neocolonialism" since the conservative regimes (it was alleged) were based on a political and economic elite which was kept in power against the wishes of the common masses by cooperating with foreign powers and enjoying their subsidies.

At the same time, American efforts to maintain good relations with revolutionary governments, chiefly the U.A.R., laid the United States open to the charge from conservative states that it was acting against their interests and without due appreciation of their friendship. Thus, whichever line the United States took aroused the ire of some Arab regimes, leading to the conclusion that America was interested only in pursuing its own welfare and not the interests of the Arab world.

The Arab-Israel conflict in 1967 precipitated these tensions in a riotous wave of anti-Americanism which swept throughout the Arab world. Not since the Boxer Rebellion in China has there been such a rapid and universal turning against a foreign power. While the American connection with Israel was the immediate cause, it was set in the wider suspicions of American intent which were already present in the Arab mind. When the mythical story was put out that American planes had assisted Israel to defeat the Arabs, it was universally believed because the Arab was prepared to believe it—not because there was any substantiating evidence. The American association with Israel combined with the hardening American attitude toward the U.A.R. since 1965 and the conviction that America did not believe that its interests would be served by a powerful, united and progressive Arab world, tended to make the charge credible. Precisely for this reason it was a useful propaganda device for the U.A.R., which hoped to temper, if not explain away, its stunning defeat by showing that it was really American strength and not Israeli arms which had made the victory.

In the immediate aftermath of the 1967 crisis the American position in the Arab world had sunk to its lowest point. Never before had American influence been less, diplomatic relations so shattered, vital interests in communications and petroleum so interrupted, and American reputation so low. American-Arab relations had gone on from hopeful expectation after the Second World War to bitter resentment and sullen hostility. Some assets remained, but they were set in a matrix of suspicion and hostility which would take a long time to disappear. The observation of one leading Arab chief-of-state in January 1967, that Arab and American objectives were so at cross-purposes that a confrontation appeared inevitable, had come true.

* * *

It seems clear that no policy of the United States in the past would have dissolved the Soviet-American, Arab-Israel and American-Arab encounters. It might more successfully have contained and moderated them in some situations, although the general nature of American objectives, commitments-in-being, and popular and congressional attitudes frequently circumscribed the freedom of American action. Once it is recognized clearly that these encounters must be lived with rather than banished, and that the American approach to the Arab world is bound by their existence, it may be possible to develop more effective policies in the future.

Chapter IX

Toward the Future

The task the United States faced in the Arab world after the 1967 debacle was not to rebuild its former position, but to work toward a new one. The collapse of American influence which accompanied the conflict made it clear that the position of the United States had not been as strong and solid as was assumed; in the hour of conflict, the persisting strains of the recurring encounters took command of the situation to wipe out many of the gains of earlier years. Not only was it impossible to return to what had been, but the former position had revealed inherent weaknesses that called into question its utility for the future.

Were the general approach and the tactical guidelines of the past still valid? The guidelines, which were never full-blown policies but only points of reference for policy formulation, had not lost their pertinency. The interests and realities out of which they arose still remained, although set in new positions and including new problems. Indeed, it was the failure more consistently to use them in approaching Arab problems which was one cause for the collapse of the American position in its hour of challenge. The decline and final cessation of significant aid to the U.A.R. after 1965 was a principal reason for President Nasser's conclusion that the United States had written off Egypt permanently as an element in its Arab policies, moving him both toward a confrontation with America and an increasing dependence on the U.S.S.R. Perhaps American aid to Egypt was unnecessarily generous from 1960 to 1964; certainly its cessation was unnecessarily drastic and did not serve American interests. Failure to be more impartial over a long period in the Arab-Israel dispute was paid for by a bitter price of broken diplomatic relations, interrupted petroleum production and transportation, and universal ill will throughout the Arab world. Directness and clarity in warning all states in the area (both the Arab states and Israel) where American interests lay, followed by appropriate action, would have averted some difficulties and given American diplomacy more weight as the 1967 crisis developed. Yet it must be remembered that the obstacles to this line of action were great and that the pressure of the Viet Nam war made it increasingly unlikely that the United States would take any strong action until it was too late.

In facing the task of building a new position on the ruins of the old, the United States must begin by rejecting the temptation to grasp at dramatic panaceas. There is no conceivable policy which will set everything right in a few months, or even in a few years, rapidly restoring American influence throughout the Arab world and resolving the threat to American interests. Only a painstaking, sustained, and steady effort, in which each gain will be minor, is possible and useful. To try to re-enter the Arab world with a flurry of new activity would weaken whatever remnants of the American position remain (since no Arab state in the aftermath of conflict could afford to be the obvious target of an American drive) and would, in any case, be impossible while diplomatic relations remain broken. This is as true for policy toward Israel as toward the Arab states; in both cases the United States has little option but to "play it cool," not yielding to pressures from either side but proceeding with deliberation and a clear view of its interests quietly to seek new relations consonant with new conditions.

It is not the purpose of this book to make detailed policy proposals for the specific issues of the day, but to point to the major problems in the large and to indicate the necessary approach to them. Of the many problems involved, three are central. The first is the future American attitude toward the revolutionary regimes of the Arab world. The traditional states have economic interests in a continued American and Western connection that are an asset in restoring some measure of the American position. Furthermore, most of these states were less directly involved in the 1967 conflict to the extent that they did not take leadership in formulating the Arab challenge to Israel but joined the fray when it became impossible for any self-respecting Arab to keep out of it. Additionally, their regimes on the whole weathered the immediate crisis better than those of some of the radical states, so that it could be argued that assisting them would further the American objective of area stability. Such considerations, backed by domestic American opinion, could easily lead to a policy of ignoring the more radical regimes and confining American attentions to the traditional states, in effect making them the "chosen instruments" of policy in the future.

For all the reasons set forth in this study, such a course would be disastrous to any hope of building a new and significant American position in the Arab world. The U.A.R. and Syria will continue to be centers of political activity, and Egyptian influence, while severely damaged, cannot be written off as a factor in future Arab affairs. One result of defeat may well be the heightening of demands for more rapid change in traditional Arab societies; the leaders and centers of radical change thus may play a larger role in the future than they have in the past. Moreover, it is in the radical states that the Soviets will try to capitalize on their gains—and where they will face their most serious dilemmas. Consequently, dealing with the entire spectrum of Arab systems—one of the tactical guidelines already discussed—is the only alternative to becoming so boxed in by identification with the conservative order that its future difficulties and possibly waning influence in Arab affairs would cut the United States off from the most significant developments of the future. Less than ever can the United States afford to polarize its position in the Arab world, becoming the champion of traditionalism (even when this is renamed "moderation") while the U.S.S.R. and radical Arab nationalists play the role of innovators and modernizers.

The second problem lies in the future relations of the United States to the Arab-Israel dispute, which is likely to continue indefinitely. Should this dispute somehow be resolved by a settlement stemming from Israel's victory or be moved by the Arabs toward a working accommodation with Israel, the problem would be less urgent—although the United States cannot expect the Arabs will forget its role in the past. But even if resolution or accommodation can take place, it will be over an extended period and not by a dramatic denouement, as Arab attitudes after the war have indicated. During the process both Israel and the Arabs will be preoccupied with what American policies will be in regard to their mutual relations and to the ultimate goal toward which the dispute may move. This means that policy toward Israel will play an even greater role in the American approach to the Arab world than it did before 1966–67, when it was possible in some cases to adopt the "ice box" policy since a conflict did not appear in the making either to American or Arab eyes.

Here the problem is the willingness and ability of the United States to resist pressure to tie it even more closely to Israel. That pressure will probably seek three objectives: more concrete commitments to Israel's defense, a renewed supply of armaments, and support for the postwar Israeli position in regard to occupied Arab territories, both on the grounds of security and as an instrument for forcing peace on the Arabs. From Israel's standpoint these objectives are in keeping with its national interests, but they are not all in keeping with the interests of the United States. More than ever it is clear that the major premise of American policy in the Middle East cannot be the protection of Israel, but must be the protection of American interests, even when this may adversely affect Israel and Arab states. In the light of the past two decades, and especially in the aftermath of the 1967 conflict, it is impossible to escape the conclusion that the special relation of the United States to Israel has served neither the specific interests of the United States in Arab countries nor the long-range objectives of American policy in the Middle East.

This is not to say that the United States should switch to a pro-Arab policy. The only valid "pro" is a "pro-American" policy, which necessarily will involve relations with both Israel and the Arab world. But these relations cannot simply be a repetition of the past; they must be defined and pursued in the new conditions following the conflict of 1967. It would be unrealistic to assume that the United States can take any action which will permanently secure Israel against renewed Arab hostility, or guarantee to the Arabs that further Israeli expansion will not take place. Some supporters of Israel argue that firm American support for Israel's continued occupation of Arab territory until direct peace negotiations are held, backed by a new commitment to the defense of Israel and an unstinted supply of arms, would bring Arab leaders to a moment of truth and force them to capitulate. There yet may be some Arabs who think that the United States has such control over Israel that it could force withdrawal of Israeli troops from Arab territory and return the situation to its *status quo ante bellum.*

Both attitudes are wishful thinking, however desirable their intended results may be. The Arabs were indeed overwhelmingly defeated in 1967, but that defeat has given no evidence of breaking the Arab will or creating the conditions for a significant Arab-Israel rapprochement. Of all people, Israelis and the world Jewish community, in view of their own history, should appreciate the dogged determination of a community to sustain hope through the centuries. The Jewish community did not forget Palestine through its long years of exile; they should not be surprised that the Arabs display a similar tenacity of memory and purpose. Two decades of Israeli existence is but a minute in the thirteen hundred years of Arab and Islamic political consciousness; other foreign kingdoms have come and gone in Palestine, and many Arabs are willing to struggle on in the conviction that Israel will go as they did.

This set of the Arab mind is encouraged by the imbalance between the resources of Israel and the Arab world. While Israel has had an advantage in effective manpower (army, technicians, administrators) during its first two decades, its population is but a tiny fraction of that of the Arab world, in which training and technical skills are steadily increasing. Moreover, in 1966 the gross national product of the Arab world was approximately nine times that of Israel. The imbalance can be expected to grow in the future as the Arab world modernizes and progresses. Arabs are thus not yet of a mind to end the struggle in a moment of temporary defeat.

On the other hand, the Arab has never understood nor truly appreciated the deep convictions on which Israel was founded, nor the determination of the Israeli to exist by right in the land of his destiny. By viewing Israel as an "imperialist" and "neo-colonial" creation, the Arab has blinded himself to its true character and underestimated the forces which make for its continued existence. Israel's hope was that an overwhelming defeat would so bring this truth home in catastrophic terms that Arab leaders would give up the struggle rather than continue a fruitless adventure. But the hope was not realized; whatever Arab accommodation might come out of the conflict, permanent peace and renunciation of future moves against Israel appear the least likely.

In this situation the United States cannot afford to take a position of irrevocable commitment to either side. It does not have the capacity to change either Arab or Israeli attitudes, or permanently to guarantee one side against the other. Commitments made in such open-end situations, where future developments are unpredictable and the risk of war ever present, can only lead to a growing and frustrating involvement, as has so clearly been demonstrated in the case of Viet Nam. Such a course would not serve American interests; the United States cannot surrender its options of action or commit its resources to the aims and policies of another state, especially a small one intent on pursuing its own aims regardless of global considerations.

It is thus not in the interest of the United States to follow a course in the future which commits it more deeply to either the Israeli or the Arab side of the dispute. To moderate the conflict and foster those influences working toward ultimate abatement is obviously in the American interest, but must be set in the framework of basic American objectives—stability, containment of Soviet influence, and protection of interests in the Arab world. This is to say that the tactical guideline of nonalignment in Middle East disputes becomes more essential than ever for approaching the problems of the Arab world.

What can the United States do? In the immediate aftermath of conflict it did not have much leverage on either Israel or the Arab states. Having confronted each other on mutually exclusive terms, the Arabs (especially the U.A.R., Jordan and Syria) and the Israelis will have to come to their own moment of reality when each party discovers that its immediate objectives cannot be realized—that the Arabs will not enter into direct negotiations, or the Israelis unconditionally withdraw. When that moment comes, the United States should support an intermediary effort, probably under international auspices. The continued closure of the Suez Canal will generate pressure on both parties from the maritime powers, and a clear indication that the United States opposes the permanent occupation of Arab land by Israel and will not assist Israel if that is its policy, may set the stage for a *modus vivendi*. Israel's concern over the Gaza strip and the Syrian borders on grounds of security must be met, but not by the annexation of these areas which will only ensure a more rapid return by the Arabs to violence and guerrilla action. With all its difficulties, a stronger United Nations presence on a much larger scale, with extensive demilitarized buffer zones adequately policed by observers, seems the most useful solution. This is the one answer to Israel's border-security problems which the Arabs could accept in their postwar mood and which could become the basis for a better adjustment to Israel in the future.

Such a solution will not please Israel, which will bitterly oppose it. But the United States has little option if it is to make the security of its own interests the primary concern of its policy. Israel must be told that its desires with respect to occupied Arab territory are secondary, so far as the United States is concerned, to the problem of coping with the new Soviet position in Arab lands. Israel cannot expect the United States to act on Israeli terms in formulating policy; America must act on American terms, even though both Israel and the Arab world will dislike it. At the same time the Arabs must have the lesson of 1967 kept before them—that the United States and other great powers will not rescue them from the results of ill-advised adventures against Israel. President Nasser maintained after his defeat that the United States had deliberately misled him by giving assurances that it would provide a peaceful solution to the dangerous impasse into which he had gotten himself. Certainly the United States tried to find a solution short of war, but it was in no position to give any binding assurances and cannot do so in the future. Both the Arabs and Israel must understand that the United States will not be a shield behind which either can machinate renewed conflict.

In the Arab world the problem of the United States is to find means to identify itself afresh with Arab development and progress. Some will say that any assistance given to an Arab government will increase its capacity to turn on Israel again, and that a public renunciation of belligerency should be the precondition of American aid. But this approach is unrealistic and would only result in keeping the door closed to possibilities of renewed American influence in Arab affairs. What the United States should seek is a new and mutually profitable relationship with Arab states, involving America in their national development and economic progress while resisting any contribution to the growth of their military capacity.

American arms sales to Arab states should be greatly restricted, if made at all. One lesson the 1967 war would appear to have taught the Arabs is that a weak society cannot successfully risk a military confrontation with a thoroughly modern one. The urge to modernize which this lesson may heighten should be used by the United States to identify itself with sound, general nonmilitary developments wherever this is possible. The course of such a policy will be painfully slow at first, but the continued utility of a Western connection and the problems the Soviets face in their new relations with the

Arab world make the task at least feasible. Arms sales to Israel, as to the Arab world, should cease so far as possible. Adding more arms either to Israeli or Arab arsenals will neither moderate nor resolve Arab-Israel hostility, and the United States cannot expect to regain influence in the area or to be effective as a mediator if it becomes a major arms dealer to either or both sides.

The pressure for arms sales to Israel arises from the conviction of many that the Soviets have committed themselves to rearming Arab states as a prelude to a fourth round of conflict. This raises the third postwar problem of American policy —its attitude and actions toward the new Soviet position in the Arab world. Some of the potentials of that position have already been indicated, but they are only potentials, and the full audit of debits and credits must await future developments.

As to arms sales, it cannot be readily assumed that the Soviets have committed themselves to replacing all the equipment lost in battle, much less to supporting an expanded Arab military establishment in the future. To be sure, immediately after the cease-fire the U.S.S.R. hastened to resupply arms, but it cannot be assumed that this level will be continued undiminished. Soviet arms policy in the future would seem to be set by three considerations: the necessity for doing enough for the Arabs to retain a posture of friendship, the securing of maximum political dividends by a minimum investment, and the necessity of avoiding an arms level which would lead their clients to undertake another ill-fated military adventure. Each of these considerations must be carefully weighed in assessing what direction Soviet policy may take. Obviously the principal Russian resource for retaining a close relation to the Arab states lies in its capacity to supply arms; it cannot supply large and sustained economic assistance except at a sacrifice which it has shown little intention of accepting. Yet the total loss in the 1967 conflict of some one billion dollars of Soviet equipment will make the Russians wary of pouring in arms in unlimited quantities. There must be more adequate dividends of influence to justify such an investment, and a greater capacity of the

Arabs to use equipment without again blackening the faces of their Soviet suppliers.

Here Soviet policy may be determined by two factors. One is the Soviet Union's own reappraisal of its interests and policies in the Arab world in the light of the lessons of the 1967 crisis and of its general strategy as a great power. The other is the inherent resistance of Arab nationalism to foreign control, which in the past has prevented the Russians from penetrating deeply into the political systems of their clients. Both factors will limit the extent to which an unlimited flood of arms would serve Soviet purposes.

It is significant that in the aftermath of the war of June 1967 the Soviets, after strongly backing the Arab position in earlier resolutions which failed of adoption by the U.N. General Assembly, consistently urged the Arabs to come to terms with the fact of Israel's existence. At the close of the session, they backed a suggestion for an American-Soviet resolution calling upon the Arabs to end their belligerency and upon the Israelis to withdraw their troops. The Soviets did not put the resolution before the Assembly, because their Arab friends would have publicly opposed it, but it was nevertheless a clear sign of Soviet moderation. The reason was not tenderness toward Israel, but realism in recognizing that another conflict would not serve Soviet interests. Having hazarded a confrontation with the United States, lost a diplomatic round in the United Nations, and revealed the limits of their support to clients in an hour of crisis, the Soviets seemed to be interested in avoiding another conflict while continuing cautiously to build up their position in Arab lands. Their support of the Security Council resolution providing for a U.N. Special Representative to help the parties seek a settlement tended to confirm that conclusion.

These considerations do not rob the flow of Soviet weapons of its danger, but they do cut the edge of the argument that the objective is to prepare the Arabs for another attack upon Israel. The Soviets can be counted upon to capitalize on the weakened American position and to utilize the tensions of the Arab world for their own benefit. But Soviet policy is above all one of *Realpolitik*—which means that its freedom of action in the Arab world is limited by commitments and interests elsewhere and must stop short of a point where it would become captive to the clients it seeks to support.

The most satisfactory answer to the arms problem would be some sort of agreement between the U.S.S.R. and the West limiting the supply of weaponry to the Arab world. This possibility was apparently raised at the Johnson-Kosygin meeting in June 1967, but without positive result. Yet it should not be assumed that the door to an arms agreement is closed for all time. It is remarkable that in the face of the Viet Nam situation and the Middle East crisis, American-Soviet relations have remained as good as they have. There is a much larger core of mutual interests in world stability than one would conclude from the public utterances of Soviet leaders. So long as the Viet Nam war continues it will be impossible for the Soviets to come to an agreement on Middle East arms; but once that conflict is resolved (or as an element in its resolution), it would not be impossible for them to consider an arrangement which would lighten their burdens in the Arab world. The United States should continue to press this possibility, recognizing that to do so involves self-restraint on its own part in not recreating the Arab-Israel arms race by immediately supplying weapons to one or both sides.

Despite the potential of the new Soviet position in the Arab world, the United States can and should change the focus of its policy from a negative checkmating of Soviet influence to a positive concern for furthering the development of Arab lands. The record makes clear that the basic danger in the Arab world has not lain so much in Soviet capabilities as in Arab weakness and disarray. Arab development (whether in its traditional or radical form), if steadily supported, will do more to assure the independence and stability of Arab states than constant American counterattacks on the Soviet position. The basic policy objective must be to secure the health of the patient, not to outdo the rival physician in prescribing nostrums until he abandons the case. The Soviets have sufficient

problems inherent in their own position, and Arab nationalism is sufficiently resistant to foreign control, to warrant the
United States' turning away from anti-Sovietism as the beginning and end of its approach to the Arab world. In the
aftermath of 1967, the American image in Arab eyes has been
that of an anti-Arab, anti-Soviet, pro-traditional force. It will
take a long time to erase this image, but the United States
cannot afford to neglect the effort. Whatever success foreign
powers can have in the Arab world in the future will be determined largely by their identification with the modernization and development of the area as an end in itself, and not
simply as an instrument in a world power struggle.

This approach may be realistic so far as the Soviet position
is concerned, but is it equally so in relation to the possible
spread of communism in the Arab world? This question cannot
be answered fully without a detailed assessment of the situation
in each country, but several legitimate general observations
can be made. One is that in no current system of Arab radical
reform have Marxists or Communist institutions been made
central. Some Soviet methods of government and economics
have been adopted, but these were selected chiefly on a pragmatic basis and not because of an ideological imperative. Arab
radicalism has been both nationalistic and pragmatic, more
interested in solving the problems of development than ad-
hering to a rigid and completely logical political or economic
system.

Another consideration is that it is hardly possible to predict
what a future "Communist" Arab state might be like. The
particular mix of Arab nationalism, social radicalism, and
communism which might emerge in some future state would
cause problems for the United States, but they would not be
the problems of dealing with an extension of the Communist
system of the Soviet Union, as the growing freedom of the
East European Communist states and the development of
their own domestic systems and policies in world affairs suggests. A Communist-tinged Arab state would be more independent of control from Moscow than many have assumed.

Moreover, the danger of the establishment of a Communist system in an Arab country would not come so much from a free choice on the part of current leaders as from a situation in which a country's dependence on the Soviet Union would be so overwhelming and irreversible as to give local Communists and their sympathizers increasing positions of power. Some observers dispute this judgment, believing that the radical leaders of the Arab world are either conscious tools or unwilling instruments of the Communist system. But to believe this is to misread the character of Arab nationalism, especially in its revolutionary phase. The revolutions of the Arab world have been expressions of an extreme stage of nationalist feeling, dedicated to complete independence from all foreign control and ending the domination of the traditional, foreign-oriented elite. The danger does not appear to lie so much in the original leaders of the Arab revolutions as in those who might come to power if their regimes and the systems of reform they instituted calamitously collapsed. Then an organized Communist minority, supported by the Soviets, might be able to seize power, owing to the chaotic state of affairs and the conviction that with the failure of "bourgeois" reform efforts the only alternative would be the full Communist system. To the extent that the Arab defeat in 1967 may shake the tenuous economic and political stability of radical Arab regimes, it can increase this possibility.

A New Mood

None of these suggested policy developments will work a quick and radical change in the American position in the Arab world. It must be said again that the problems are too deep, the impact of the 1967 crisis too pervasive, to make possible a rapid return of American influence. And none of the suggestions is a radical departure from the tactical guidelines of the American approach which have been used spasmodically during the last decade. What they call for is a more sustained use of the guidelines as a basis for American policy. The nature of American interests, the characteristics of the Arab world, and the instruments of diplomacy available to the United States continue their essential character, despite the new circumstances. When American policy has gone astray, it has been because it undertook commitments not related to its interests, became partisan where it should have been even-handed, and failed to sustain its long-range objectives through the stresses of immediate situations. To avoid such actions in the future is an essential ingredient for success in the task of creating a new American position.

It is the mood in which policies toward the Arab world have been made that must change. The attitudes toward Arab affairs built up in the past deeply infect the atmosphere in which the policy-maker weighs the problems of the future. Unencumbered by these, able to survey the scene for what it is rather than for what it was, he must approach the challenge of the future with a freshness of outlook which too often has been absent. This is what the American approach to the Arab world most needs—an open mind and a more confident spirit, less irritation, and more disposition to work steadily toward ultimate goals. The momentum of the past too easily dominates the direction of the future; new problems are faced as though they were old, old solutions offered as though they were new. A change in mood to fit the change in times is the most essential requirement for the United States in dealing successfully with Arab affairs.

What should this new mood be? Its first element is a more deliberate patience—steadily pursued effort with eyes fixed on ultimate objectives rather than always distracted by im-mediate problems. Steadiness in particularly needed in dealing with the Middle East, where change is rapid and continuous, stability tenuous, political leadership uncertain, and national policies compounded more of emotion than of rationality. In such a situation quick returns on a policy investment are few. It is only by sustaining a judicious course of action through an extended period that it can be effective. Neither revolutionary nor traditional governments are apt to respond to a foreign initiative as quickly as Americans expect. The first are changing too rapidly, the second too slowly, to move in the desired direction at a pace which immediately justifies the policy being used. Only persistent and sustained effort, undeflected by the vagaries of daily developments, can possibly result in lasting influence.

Too frequently in the past American policies have been characterized by the same headlong expediency of which President Nasser is often accused—reaction rather than action. Problems in the Arab world have been constant and numerous, but they cannot be dealt with successfully by alternate waves of activity and impatience, or simply by saying: "Go see what the Arabs are doing and tell them to stop it."

Here the United States would do well to ponder the record of the Soviet Union. Although the Soviets have operated under most of the restrictions which have beset America in the Arab world, lack some of the instruments of power the United States possesses, and have encountered setbacks in sustaining and explaining their influence, they have displayed a persistence in maintaining their Arab relations which has become one of the chief assets of their country's position. This is not because they have a more consistent foreign policy; like the United States their course in the Middle East has been marked by pragmatism, change, and contradiction. But they have been more willing than the United States to maintain good relations through periods of stress, providing their continued presence, extended contacts, and sustained assistance to win friends and influence people. The focus of their view appears longer than ours, their reliance on patient persistence greater.

The second element in the new mood is that of realism—estimating conditions for what they are, differentiating between interests and desiderata, appraising accurately the forces in the Arab world and not viewing them simply in the light of a popular or traditional image. A fresh evaluation of the capacity of the various centers of power is constantly needed. In the aftermath of the 1967 crisis, all the power factors of the Middle East underwent some change. The Soviets had new opportunities opened to them, which some observers wishfully devalued, yet at the same time they faced new problems which could inhibit their ability to make further permanent gains. American policy cannot be based either on underestimating the strength of the new Soviet position, or on overestimating the ease with which they may capitalize on it.

Nor is it possible in the aftermath of 1967 to maintain that the U.A.R. and its radical regime can dominate the Arab world. The capacity of revolutionary Egypt to gather the other Arab states under its wing has always been less than many have assumed, and the vision of an Egyptian empire stretching from the Valley of the Nile to the Persian Gulf was generated more by the fears of the West than the realities of the Middle East. Even before the 1967 defeat, it was clear that Egypt had neither the resources nor the capacity permanently to dominate the area. After defeat, with its economy shattered, its army proved wanting, its military leadership of Arab forces revealed as ineffective, and its relations with sister Arab states again thrown in turmoil, it faced a bleak future. Yet it would be unrealistic to write off the U.A.R. as of little importance in future Arab affairs. Its activism, although possibly curtailed by the experience of defeat, will continue to make it an influence in Arab affairs while its revolutionary goals will persist in their appeal to the discontented in neighboring Arab states. But the problem must be seen for what it is—a matter of intermittent interference and influence rather than of growing expansion likely to result in permanent control of the Arab world.

The reappraisal of American-Arab-Israel relations has already been covered in the previous chapter. Realism demands that the United States be more honest with itself in recognizing the problems for American interests in Arab lands caused by its history of special relationship to Israel. Whether it is possible to change the relationship in view of the urgency of the post-1967 situation will depend partly on Israel's supporters in the United States, who can no longer assume that American and Israeli interests are inevitably parallel, partly on elected officials who are willing to make American interests take precedence over a popular election issue, and partly on the administration's determination to pursue American interests in the Arab world in the face of recurring public pressure.

Above all, realism demands that the United States shall more accurately estimate the limitations of its power to control Arab affairs. Every time a new crisis breaks out there will be those who take it as a confirmation of passivity in American policy, or timidity in the use of American power. Less than ever after the 1967 crisis can any foreign power assume it has the power to police the Middle East or even to control its own clients there. The United States cannot expect more of its foreign policy than the instruments of diplomacy at its command make possible, and in the aftermath of 1967 these instruments were not strong.

The mood compounded of patience and realism is, in effect, a mood of sophistication in formulating and conducting foreign policy. To many Americans, sophistication is suspect; it suggests deception, specious argument, a wily course of action without principle or consistency. But this is an unwarranted connotation identifying the word with "sophistry" rather than with "wisdom," which is what the Greek root means. A sophisticated foreign policy is one which deals with things as they are, which accepts the necessity of diverse courses of action at different times (or at the same time) without belaboring every supposed departure from consistency, and which understands and makes place for the attitudes and responses of other nations even when we do not approve of them. Thus, a sophisticated policy need be neither devoid of principles nor in contradiction to them, but it must be one which recognizes that rarely in the Middle East is the balance of factors in a situation so overwhelming that one side can be fully supported and the other completely neglected.

This kind of approach has not been the hallmark of many American policies toward the Arab world. Too often problems have been approached in simple, moralistic terms, as when Secretary Dulles predicted that the nationalization of the Suez Canal would fail because he believed that the moral forces of the world would rally against it.

This may seem an exaggerated view of the American position, or more accurately of the mood in which many American positions have been taken. Yet a senior official in the Department of State mentioned to a group discussing Middle Eastern affairs the near hopelessness of obtaining public or congressional support for sophisticated policies in that area. To accept that limitation on American policy is to say in effect that American interests in the Middle East cannot adequately be protected. No one knowing the area can be under the delusion that there are simple answers to its problems. The inner contradictions of Arab politics are too deep, the tempo of change too rapid, the disparity of interests between individual states too great, to be encompassed by anything but a flexible and sophisticated approach.

Under the Kennedy administration, the American approach to the Arab world began to develop a greater degree of sophistication. The guidelines reviewed in this study reflected a fresh appreciation of Arab affairs and the courses of action which could be applied to them. Some of the dilemmas involved could be faced with equanimity because they were only incidental to the long-range objectives of American policy. But it has been hard to maintain this sophistication: weariness on the part of policy-makers, pressure of other issues, and renewed disorder in the Arab world changed the mood to one of sharpened reaction and growing impatience. The problem for the future is whether the United States can rise above the irritations and frustrations which came to a head in the 1967 crisis to pursue more calmly, deliberately and maturely its objectives in the Arab world.

Index

COUNCIL ON FOREIGN RELATIONS

Officers and Directors

PUBLICATIONS

FOREIGN AFFAIRS (quarterly), edited by Hamilton Fish Armstrong.

THE UNITED STATES IN WORLD AFFAIRS (annual). Volumes for 1931, 1932 and 1933, by Walter Lippmann and William O. Scroggs; for 1934–1935, 1936, 1937, 1938, 1939 and 1940, by Whitney H. Shepardson and William O. Scroggs; for 1945–1947, 1947–1948 and 1948–1949, by John C. Campbell; for 1949, 1950, 1951, 1952, 1953 and 1954, by Richard P. Stebbins; for 1955, by Hollis W. Barber; for 1956, 1957, 1958, 1959, 1960, 1961, 1962 and 1963, by Richard P. Stebbins; for 1964, by Jules Davids; for 1965 and 1966, by Richard P. Stebbins.

DOCUMENTS OF AMERICAN FOREIGN RELATIONS (annual). Volume for 1952 edited by Clarence W. Baier and Richard P. Stebbins; for 1953 and 1954 edited by Peter V. Curl; for 1955, 1956, 1957, 1958 and 1959 edited by Paul E. Zinner; for 1960, 1961, 1962 and 1963 edited by Richard P. Stebbins; for 1964 by Jules Davids; for 1965 and 1966, by Richard P. Stebbins.

POLITICAL HANDBOOK AND ATLAS OF THE WORLD (annual), edited by Walter H. Mallory.

HOW NATIONS BEHAVE: LAW AND FOREIGN POLICY, by Louis Henkin (1968).

THE INSECURITY OF NATIONS, by Charles W. Yost (1968).

PROSPECTS FOR SOVIET SOCIETY, edited by Allen Kassof (1968).

THE AMERICAN APPROACH TO THE ARAB WORLD, by John S. Badeau (1968).

U.S. POLICY AND THE SECURITY OF ASIA, by Fred Greene (1968).

NEGOTIATING WITH THE CHINESE COMMUNISTS: THE U.S. EXPERIENCE, by Kenneth T. Young (1968).

FROM ATLANTIC TO PACIFIC: A NEW INTEROCEAN CANAL, by Immanuel J. Klette (1967).

TITO'S SEPARATE ROAD: America and Yugoslavia in World Politics, by John C. Campbell (1967).

U.S. TRADE POLICY: New Legislation for the Next Round, by John W. Evans (1967).

TRADE LIBERALIZATION AMONG INDUSTRIAL COUNTRIES: Objectives and Alternatives, by Bela Balassa (1967).

THE CHINESE PEOPLE'S LIBERATION ARMY, by Brig. General Samuel B. Griffith II U.S.M.C. (ret.) (1967).

THE ARTILLERY OF THE PRESS: Its Influence on American Foreign Policy, by James Reston (1967).

ATLANTIC ECONOMIC COOPERATION: The Case of the O.E.C.D., by Henry G. Aubrey (1967).

TRADE, AID AND DEVELOPMENT: The Rich and Poor Nations, by John Pincus (1967).

BETWEEN TWO WORLDS: Policy, Press and Public Opinion on Asian–American Relations, by John Hohenberg (1967).

THE CONFLICTED RELATIONSHIP: The West and the Transformation of Asia, Africa and Latin America, by Theodore Geiger (1966).

THE ATLANTIC IDEA AND ITS EUROPEAN RIVALS, by H. van B. Cleveland (1966).

EUROPEAN UNIFICATION IN THE SIXTIES: From the Veto to the Crisis, by Miriam Camps (1966).

THE UNITED STATES AND CHINA IN WORLD AFFAIRS, by Robert Blum, edited by A. Doak Barnett (1966).

THE FUTURE OF THE OVERSEAS CHINESE IN SOUTHEAST ASIA, by Lea A. Williams (1966).

THE CONSCIENCE OF THE RICH NATIONS: The Development Assistance

Committee and the Common Aid Effort, by Seymour J. Rubin (1966).

ATLANTIC AGRICULTURAL UNITY: Is it Possible?, by John O. Coppock (1966).

TEST BAN AND DISARMAMENT: The Path of Negotiation, by Arthur H. Dean (1966).

COMMUNIST CHINA'S ECONOMIC GROWTH AND FOREIGN TRADE, by Alexander Eckstein (1966).

POLICIES TOWARD CHINA: Views from Six Continents, edited by A. M. Halpern (1966).

THE AMERICAN PEOPLE AND CHINA, by A. T. Steele (1966).

INTERNATIONAL POLITICAL COMMUNICATION, by W. Phillips Davison (1965).

MONETARY REFORM FOR THE WORLD ECONOMY, by Robert V. Roosa (1965).

AFRICAN BATTLELINE: American Policy Choices in Southern Africa, by Waldemar A. Nielsen (1965).

NATO IN TRANSITION: The Future of the Atlantic Alliance, by Timothy W. Stanley (1965).

REMNANTS OF EMPIRE: The United Nations and the End of Colonialism, by David W. Wainhouse (1965).

ALTERNATIVE TO PARTITION: For a Broader Conception of America's Role in Europe, by Zbigniew Brzezinski (1965).

THE TROUBLED PARTNERSHIP: A Re-Appraisal of the Atlantic Alliance, by Henry A. Kissinger (1965).

THE EUROPEAN COMMUNITY AND AMERICAN TRADE: A Study in Atlantic Economics and Policy, by Randall Hinshaw (1964).

THE FOURTH DIMENSION OF FOREIGN POLICY: Educational and Cultural Affairs, by Phillip H. Coombs (1964).

AMERICAN AGENCIES INTERESTED IN INTERNATIONAL AFFAIRS (Fifth Edition), compiled by Donald Wasson (1964).

JAPAN AND THE UNITED STATES IN WORLD TRADE, by Warren S. Hunsberger (1964).

FOREIGN AFFAIRS BIBLIOGRAPHY, 1952–1962, by Henry L. Roberts (1964).

THE DOLLAR IN WORLD AFFAIRS: An Essay in International Financial Policy, by Henry G. Aubrey (1964).

ON DEALING WITH THE COMMUNIST WORLD, by George F. Kennan (1964).

FOREIGN AID AND FOREIGN POLICY, by Edward S. Mason (1964).

THE SCIENTIFIC REVOLUTION AND WORLD POLITICS, by Caryl P. Haskins (1964).

AFRICA: A Foreign Affairs Reader, edited by Philip W. Quigg (1964).

THE PHILIPPINES AND THE UNITED STATES: Problems of Partnership, by George E. Taylor (1964).

SOUTHEAST ASIA IN UNITED STATES POLICY, by Russell H. Fifield (1963).

UNESCO: ASSESSMENT AND PROMISE, by George N. Shuster (1963).

THE PEACEFUL ATOM IN FOREIGN POLICY, by Arnold Kramish (1963).

THE ARABS AND THE WORLD: Nasser's Arab Nationalist Policy, by Charles D. Cremeans (1963).

TOWARD AN ATLANTIC COMMUNITY, by Christian A. Herter (1963).

THE SOVIET UNION, 1922–1962: A Foreign Affairs Reader, edited by Philip E. Mosley (1963).

THE POLITICS OF FOREIGN AID: American Experience in Southeast Asia, by John D. Montgomery (1962).

SPEARHEADS OF DEMOCRACY: Labor in the Developing Countries, by George C. Lodge (1962).

LATIN AMERICA: Diplomacy and Reality, by Adolf A. Berle (1962).

THE ORGANIZATION OF AMERICAN STATES AND THE HEMISPHERE CRISIS, by John C. Dreier (1962).

THE UNITED NATIONS: Structure for Peace, by Ernest A. Gross (1962).

THE LONG POLAR WATCH: Canada and the Defense of North America, by Melvin Conant (1962).

ARMS AND POLITICS IN LATIN AMERICA (Revised Edition), by Edwin Lieuwen (1961).

THE FUTURE OF UNDERDEVELOPED COUNTRIES: Political Implications of Economic Development (Revised Edition), by Eugene Staley (1961).

SPAIN AND DEFENSE OF THE WEST: Ally and Liability, by Arthur P. Whitaker (1961).

SOCIAL CHANGE IN LATIN AMERICA TODAY: Its Implications for United States Policy, by Richard N. Adams, John P. Gillin, Allan R. Holmberg, Oscar Lewis, Richard W. Patch, and Charles W. Wagley (1961).

FOREIGN POLICY: THE NEXT PHASE: The 1960s (Revised Edition), by Thomas K. Finletter (1960).

DEFENSE OF THE MIDDLE EAST: Problems of American Policy (Revised Edition), by John C. Campbell (1960).

COMMUNIST CHINA AND ASIA: Challenge to American Policy, by A. Doak Barnett (1960).

FRANCE, TROUBLED ALLY: De Gaulle's Heritage and Prospects, by Edgar S. Furniss, Jr. (1960).

THE SCHUMAN PLAN: A Study in Economic Cooperation 1950–1959, by William Diebold, Jr. (1959).

Soviet Economic Aid: The New Aid and Trade Policy in Underdeveloped Countries, by Joseph S. Berliner (1958).

NATO and The Future of Europe, by Ben T. Moore (1958).

India and America: A Study of Their Relations, by Phillips Talbot and S. L. Poplai (1958).

Nuclear Weapons and Foreign Policy, by Henry A. Kissinger (1957).

Moscow-Peking Axis: Strength and Strains, by Howard L. Boorman, Alexander Eckstein, Philip S. Mosely, and Benjamin Schwartz (1957).

Russia and America: Dangers and Prospects, by Henry L. Roberts (1956).

70 71 72 73   12 11 10 9 8 7 6 5 4 3